How To keep on smoking and live

*The Earliest Representation of a Tobacco Plant and
The Operation of Smoking*

From Petro Pena and Matthia de LoBell (MEDICI),
Nova Stirpium Adversaria Lantwerp, 1576

How to keep on smoking and live

By
Roger Williams Harris

St. Martin's Press
New York

Copyright © 1978 by Roger Williams Harris
All rights reserved. For information, write:
St. Martin's Press, Inc.
175 Fifth Ave.
New York, N.Y. 10010.
Manufactured in the United States of America
Library of Congress Catalog Card Number: 77-99128

Library of Congress Cataloging in Publication Data

Harris, Roger Williams.
  How to keep on smoking and live.

  Bibliography: p.
  1. Smoking. 2. Cigarette habit. I. Title.
HV5740.H37   1978   613.8'5   77-99128

ISBN 0-312-39594-9
ISBN 0-312-39595-7 pbk.

COVER DESIGN BY JOHN RENFER, BOSTON

This book is written for, and dedicated to, all the smokers who have tried to quit or cut down – and failed.

ACKNOWLEDGEMENTS

The following illustrations were included through the courtesy of George G. Harrap & Company Ltd. of London, publishers of "A History of Smoking" by Count Egon Caesar Corti in whose book these rare prints appeared:

The Earliest Representation of a Tobacco Plant
Maya Priest Smoking
Smoke as a Cure for Illness
Drinking and Smoking Bout in Amsterdam
Popularity of Cigar-Smoking in London, 1827.

CONTENTS

Introduction

PART I
THE SECOND-BEST SMOKING PLAN

1. The Fumer Fallacy
2. Rules Are Tools
3. Phase I
4. Phase II
5. Phase III
6. Phase IV
7. Phase V
8. Phase VI The Happy Hookah

PART II
ON THE SUBJECT OF QUITTING

1. Smoker's Self-Testing Kit
2. Trick Or Trachea
3. A Cigar Or Pipe Won't Make It Right
4. And Now Something Special for the Ladies
5. Is There Such A Thing As Will Power And Why Is Mine Missing?
6. Now That You're Comfortable — Quit
7. Don't Sit Back and Relapse

PART III
MOST EVERYTHING YOU NEVER WANTED TO KNOW ABOUT CIGARETTES AND DIDN'T KNOW WHO TO ASK

1. Puff! The Magic Drag On
2. Malice In Wonderland

3. $moke Gets In Their Ayes
4. Pit Stop On Tobacco Road
5. Smoke Rings From The Doom Fumes

Bibliography

Tar and Nicotine Content of 166 Varieties of Cigarettes
    Alphabetical Listing By Brand Name
    Listed By Increasing Order Of Tar Values

Canadian Cigarettes — Average "Tar" And Nicotine

INTRODUCTION

"**Expert:** A man who knows 47 ways to make love but doesn't know any girls."

Most of the books and articles one reads on the subject of smoking appear to be written by tobacco experts who never smoked cigarettes. First, they try to scare the hell out of you . . . "Let me describe in 4-color detail the inside lining of a smoker's lung after 30 years on 2 packs a day . . ." Then, after giving us the old medical one-two, they offer suggestions for cutting down which only a cigarette virgin would seriously voice in public.

"Stop Inhaling."

This compares to asking a cigarette smoker to stop breathing. What in the world do they think we smoke for — our health?

"Smoke only half the cigarette."

We would be happy to smoke only half of each cigarette, but unfortunately the act of smoking is such an unconscious process that we aren't usually aware that we light up in the first place. Now, if you could build a little gun powder into the paper about half way down. . . .

"Take fewer draws on each cigarette."

Same answer. Not all, but most of the cigarettes

11

we smoke get removed from the pack, placed in the mouth, lit, smoked, snuffed out, and all the while we are only vaguely aware it happened.

This is a different kind of book, written by a cigarette smoker who put himself through the process described in Part I and suddenly realized he had discovered something important. He proceeded to ask friends who smoked to follow the same regime. Most succeeded. Some, however, failed. Investigation revealed that they had not read the instructions carefully and had not followed the rules.

The procedure itself couldn't be simpler. But let's face it. You're hooked on cigarettes and changing your tar and nicotine intake has got to be done gradually. I guarantee you will be taking in up to 90% less tar and nicotine within the next 4 to 8 weeks. (It depends on which level you are starting from.) But that guarantee will only hold if: (1) you put aside any preconceived ideas on the subject; (2) you read the chapters in Part I *carefully* and *thoughtfully;* and, (3) you follow directions. Thousands of smokers have done this successfully. One of the results that surprises and pleases them most is the realization that the change is permanent. They have reduced their tar and nicotine intake by up to 90%, they still enjoy the same amount of cigarette smoking, and they have no desire to go back to their original tar and nicotine level.

Read carefully. Follow the directions. Don't try to jump ahead and speed up the process. You will almost surely fail. The temptation then will be to blame the plan rather than yourself. Nothing will be accomplished.

Take your time. You are doing something that is extremely important, even vital, for you and your health. It is certainly worth following the rules for 4 to 8 weeks to achieve a vastly improved smoking level for the rest of your life or until you take the next step and quit.

PART I
THE SECOND-BEST SMOKING PLAN

"My interest is in the future — because I am going to spend the rest of my life there."

Charles F. Kettering

1

THE FUMER FALLACY

"It has been my experience that folks who have no vices have very few virtues."

Abraham Lincoln

Part I of this book is all about THE SECOND-BEST SMOKING PLAN. The *best* smoking plan in the world, of course, is to quit cold right now. It is all too easy to list the reasons why:
1. You will stop endangering your health.
2. You will save money.
3. You won't have to carry matches and cigarettes everywhere you go.
4. You are less likely to burn down your house.
5. You will no longer have throat irritation and smoker's cough.
6. If you don't smoke, there's a far better chance your kids won't smoke.
7. Your sense of taste and smell will improve.
8. You will almost certainly live longer.

Okay. You know all the reasons, but you don't intend to quit, at least not today. Perhaps you heard the story about the man who quit smoking and substituted chewing on toothpicks; it's reported he died of Dutch Elm Disease. A droll story if smoking were not such a serious subject.

So, you are ready for THE SECOND-BEST SMOKING PLAN. There is a simple, beautiful logic to this smoking plan. To wit, if you are going to be a damn fool and smoke cigarettes for another year or another ten years, why not do so with the least possible damage to your health.

Aha! you say; the only way to do that is to cut way down on the number of cigarettes per day. So, you tried this, and you couldn't or didn't want to stick with such a regime. But that is not what this smoking plan is all about.

All right, the only other way to drastically cut down on your intake of tar and nicotine is to smoke some super-mild cigarette or use some crazy type of filter. You have tried all of these and couldn't stand it because you could hardly taste the cigarette. It was like smoking warm air.

Now we are getting to the heart of the matter. Breathes there a smoker anywhere who has not, at least once, read the ads or the warnings and rushed out to purchase a milder cigarette than his present brand. Perhaps he smoked his way through two or even three packs before throwing in the towel — no taste, no strength, no smoke.

Chances are that you have done this on more than one occasion. After giving it a good try, you couldn't wait to get back to your old satisfying brand. The most serious damage caused by this experience was to establish a precedent in your mind that is entirely false but very persuasive. This is known as *The Fumer Fallacy*. *Fumer* is French for "to smoke" which tells you something about the word fumes.

The Fumer Fallacy operates as follows: The

smoker tries a milder cigarette, finds it unsatisfying, *and believes this milder cigarette will continue to be just as unsatisfying tomorrow, the day after tomorrow, next week, forever.*

Ipso facto – there is no point in changing to a less harmful cigarette because it will always taste as though you were smoking through a mattress. It is almost worse than not smoking at all. A discouraging premise indeed, but totally incorrect and precisely the reason most smokers fail to stay with a milder cigarette. They simply don't realize that it takes four or five days, or in some cases a week or two, to get fully acclimated to a lower tar and nicotine level.

If a smoker tries the big switch to a brand that is 15 to 20 milligrams lower in tar, he can hardly taste anything. It is almost as if he quit smoking completely, which is obviously not his intention. Do not attempt such a large reduction. It rarely succeeds.

Remember also that the very act of changing to a different brand, any brand, is a wrench. We are all very comfortable with and almost sensually attached to our regular brand. Saying goodbye to it is, quite literally, the end of a love affair. Happily, you will be just as much in love with your new brand when you complete THE SECOND-BEST SMOKING PLAN.

You can reduce your intake of tar and nicotine by up to 90% and still enjoy smoking as much as ever. If you presently smoke 20 cigarettes a day, you can continue to smoke 20 cigarettes a day, but it will be the equivalent of 2 or 3 of your former brand.

How important is this to you?

Not too long ago, an ad-hoc group of scientists reviewed the latest data on smoking at the request of the

Surgeon General. Among their conclusions were the following:

1. The preponderance of scientific evidence strongly suggests that the lower the "tar" and nicotine content of cigarette smoke, the less harmful would be the effect.
2. The potential benefit to the individual consumer who might shift to a lower tar and nicotine cigarette would be negated if this shift were accompanied by an increase in the number of cigarettes consumed, or in the length of each cigarette used. There is evidence that, by and large, this does *not* occur; that the shift to low "tar" and nicotine cigarettes tends to be accompanied by the same level of consumption or an even lower level rather than by an increased consumption.

That last sentence surprises people who have not tried THE SECOND-BEST SMOKING PLAN. On the surface, it appears logical that with a low tar and nicotine cigarette the smoker will want to light up more frequently, but this is not necessarily the case. As you acclimate to a lower level, the urge to smoke usually diminishes. Even if you should establish a temporary pattern of a few extra cigarettes each day, your tar and nicotine level is so much lower that you are still far better off.

In September, 1976 the American Cancer Society published the results of a 12-year study which for the first time documented a lower death rate among smokers of low-tar cigarettes vs. smokers of medium or high-tar cigarettes. This was a definitive piece of research and has great significance for the reader of this book who successfully follows THE SECOND-BEST SMOKING PLAN.

The statement by the ad-hoc committee, mentioned previously, used the term "strongly suggests" which hinted that their conclusion about low-tar cigarettes might be incorrect. The major counter-speculations were:

1. That smokers of low-tar brands might increase their consumption. This turned out not to be the case.
2. Smokers of low-tar cigarettes might inhale the smoke more deeply. If so, then their effective exposure to tar and nicotine might not be reduced while their exposure to gases in cigarette smoke might be increased.
3. It could be that gases contained in cigarette smoke are as harmful if not more harmful than the tar and nicotine content of the smoke. An increase in carbon monoxide might increase the risk of coronary heart disease.

Therefore, if all this is true, the net effect of reduction in tar and nicotine might be an *increase* in age-related death rates.

In 1959, the American Cancer Society set out to find an answer. Volunteer workers for the American Cancer Society enrolled over 1,000,000 men and women in a prospective study. Upon enrollment, each subject answered a lengthy questionnaire. During the first 6 years, enrollment and tracing of subjects was conducted in 1,121 counties in 25 states. At the end of the second 6-year period (June, 1972) the researchers were still able to gather data from nearly 850,000 of the original participants.

For the purposes of this report, the researchers defined high-tar cigarettes as containing 25.8 to 35.7 mg. tar. Low-tar cigarettes delivered 17.6 mg. tar or less. Today a 17.6 mg. tar cigarette is not considered low tar. In fact it is about the average, but in 1960 when the study began, there were far fewer low-tar brands. This is an extremely important point to keep in mind as you contemplate the result of this study. When you complete THE SECOND-BEST SMOKING PLAN, the tar level of each cigarette will be 1 mg. or less. In other words, *you will be smoking at a far lower level than the control group in this study who were designated as low-tar smokers.*

For men and women in both time periods, the results were as follows:

ADJUSTED NUMBER OF DEATHS Total Deaths				
Sex	Period	"High" T/N	"Medium" T/N	"Low" T/N
Male	1960-1966	1,543.0	1,394.4	1,351.7
Male	1966-1972	935.2	913.7	759.4
Female	1960-1966	1,253.6	1,117.1	1,053.9
Female	1966-1972	1,003.7	874.7	826.2
	TOTAL	4,735.5	4,299.9	3,991.2
TABLE 1				

The adjusted number of deaths among smokers of "low-tar" cigarettes was 16% lower than among smokers of "high-tar" cigarettes.

ADJUSTED NUMBER OF DEATHS
Lung Cancer Deaths

Sex	Period	"High" T/N	"Medium" T/N	"Low" T/N
Male	1960-1966	122.4	117.4	101.0
Male	1966-1972	89.6	84.5	70.6
Female	1960-1966	48.3	41.4	27.4
Female	1966-1972	58.1	42.2	36.2
	TOTAL	318.4	285.5	235.2

TABLE 2

The adjusted number of lung cancer deaths among smokers of "low-tar" cigarettes was 26% lower than among smokers of "high-tar" cigarettes.

ADJUSTED NUMBER OF DEATHS
Coronary Heart Disease

Sex	Period	"High" T/N	"Medium" T/N	"Low" T/N
Male	1960-1966	696.5	632.5	645.6
Male	1966-1972	336.0	345.6	274.2
Female	1960-1966	318.7	277.5	257.4
Female	1966-1972	265.6	228.0	215.5
	TOTAL	1,616.8	1,483.3	1,392.7

TABLE 3

The adjusted number of deaths from coronary heart disease among smokers of "low-tar" cigarettes was 14% lower than smokers of "high-tar" cigarettes.

It should also be noted that death rates (from all combined causes of death) were considerably higher in subjects who smoked "low-tar" cigarettes than in subjects who never smoked regularly. So, while the study proves conclusively that "low-tar" cigarettes (in this study 17.6 mg. or lower) are less dangerous, they can in no way be considered "safe" cigarettes. There may never be such a thing as a "safe" cigarette, but if you follow this smoking plan to its conclusion, you will be smoking with full satisfaction at the nearest possible safe level available today.

Before plunging into the plan at your current tar and nicotine level, please review this chapter with particular attention to The Fumer Fallacy. And remember, you *will* adjust to a lower tar and nicotine level; you *will* be surprised at how quickly this is accomplished, and you *will* continue to enjoy your cigarette smoking just as much.

2

RULES ARE TOOLS

"Health is a crown on a well man's head, but no one can see it but a sick man."

Egyptian Proverb

Don't let the rules and suggestions that follow deceive you as unimportant. They are the result of much testing and observation.

THE SECOND-BEST SMOKING PLAN has four basic rules:

1. *Sample*
2. *Invest*
3. *No Substitutes*
4. *Acclimate.*

After testing the plan for 5 years on a variety of smokers, these 4 steps evolved as the most effective procedures. They are uncomplicated but crucial to your success.

Approximately 8 out of 10 smokers will find themselves in Phase I or Phase II as a starting point. Each Phase groups a number of popular cigarette brands which fall in a specific tar content range. If you should not find your present brand in one of the Phases, check the United States government listing in the back of the book to determine your starting point. Canadian cigarette brands are also listed.

RULE 1. SAMPLE

Consider the various brands in the next Phase ahead of you. It is very helpful to buy a pack of 3 or 4 of these lower tar and nicotine brands. Sample each of them and determine which one you want to smoke while you acclimate yourself to this lower level.

RULE 2. INVEST

When you have made your selection, *purchase at least 2 cartons* of that brand. If you are a 2-pack-a-day-or-more smoker, buy 4 cartons of your selected brand.

There are two good reasons for purchasing that many cartons:

a. As a financial commitment to your serious intentions, and
b. Because these milder brands are not generally available in vending machines or restaurants, nor are they usually available from another smoker. Which brings us to Rule 3.

RULE 3. NO SUBSTITUTES

It is extremely important that you do not run out of your new brand and substitute even a single stronger cigarette during this readjustment period. Such a digression can undo all your progress and send you right back to "Start."

RULE 4. ACCLIMATE

(a) Smoke your new brand *exclusively* until the cartons are nearly finished. Somewhere between the first and second weeks, you should be completely acclimated to your new milder cigarette. (b) At this point, if you are feeling confident and thoroughly satisfied with your new brand, you are ready to move on to the next Phase at a lower tar and nicotine level. (c) If you don't feel 100% ready to move to the next Phase, purchase 2 or 3 more cartons in preparation for this next step.

It is not surprising that the heavier smoker takes considerably longer to adjust. But he does eventually adjust and with just as much satisfaction at his new lower smoking level as the lighter smoker who simply gets there a little sooner.

The rate of your tar reduction will be greatly enhanced if you avoid the "long" 100 mm. plus cigarettes. The tobacco industry appears to be involved in a devious and dangerous game with the smoker's health. First, they establish a king size brand, and then market it again in the 100 mm. length. There are cases where smokers who had achieved complete satisfaction with, for example, king size Carltons at 1 mg. tar, switched to 100 mm. Carlton Longs at 5 mg. tar. They thereby increase their tar, nicotine and gas intake by as much as 500%.

It is important to remember that when you smoke a cigarette the tobacco nearest the filter steadily collects tar and nicotine as the smoke passes through. Consequently, the last three or four puffs on a cigarette are the most dangerous and damaging. The longer the cigarette, the greater the threat. King size cigarettes are what the name signifies, oversized cigarettes that last a satisfactory length of time for one smoke. The same brand in the 100 mm. length is far more insidious. Stay with the king size exclusively.

Don't get discouraged if you don't acclimate as quickly as you would like. Smokers vary widely in physical and psychological terms. Some people breeze through THE SECOND-BEST SMOKING PLAN in half the usual time with no uncomfortable adjustments. Others have to struggle a little at the beginning of each Phase. Remember that all kinds of smokers have used this plan with great success, *if they stayed with the rules*.

During the first few days and weeks with your new brand, you may perhaps light up more frequently. This is quite common and generally temporary. As you proceed through this plan, greatly reducing your intake of tar and nicotine, you will almost certainly, in time, desire fewer, not more, cigarettes per day.

Occasionally, people experience greater coughing in the morning during the first few days with a new brand. Again, this is only temporary and appears to result from the irritation of a different make of cigarette. Hundreds of smokers who have completed the plan report that one of the earliest benefits they enjoy is far less throat irritation and coughing.

3

PHASE I

"A man's best friend is his dogma."

Franklin P. Adams

If your regular cigarette brand falls in the Phase I category, you have the furthest to go and *the most to gain.* Your brand is one of the strongest cigarettes manufactured in the United States. Chances are you are also a somewhat heavier smoker, well over a pack a day and quite possibly in the deadly area of 2 or 3 packs a day. All the more reason to start THE SECOND-BEST SMOKING PLAN at once, and all the more reason you will derive the greatest benefits.

"Based on the mounting statistical evidence from several studies, it seems clear that a man who smokes 2 packages of cigarettes or more a day has about 1 chance in 10 of eventually developing lung cancer. A man who smokes less than a pack a day has about 1 chance in 270 of developing it." — 10th Annual Report, Mass. Div. of American Cancer Society.

As mentioned in the previous chapter, the heavy smoker may have a slightly more difficult time getting started with a somewhat milder cigarette. He or she is more susceptible to The Fumer Fallacy. Once you break through that deception and discover how quickly and painlessly you can adapt to a modest reduction in your tar and nicotine intake, you will move through the rest of the plan with full confidence.

Review the rules again and set sail for those calmer and safer waters common sense dictates your destination should be.

PHASE I
NON-MENTHOL
KING SIZE SOFT PACK NON-FILTER

	Mg. Tar	Mg. Nicotine
Raleigh	24	1.4
Philip Morris Commander	24	1.4
Old Gold Straights	25	1.5
Pall Mall	26	1.6
Herbert Tareyton	28	1.8
Stratford	29	1.1
Fatima	29	1.7
Chesterfield	29	1.7
Domino	33	1.4

PHASE I
MENTHOL

	Size	*Mg. Tar*	*Mg. Nicotine*
L.T. Brown (Filter)	120mm.	19	1.4
Newport (Filter)	100mm.	20	1.4
Kool (Non-Filter)	Reg.	21	1.3
More (Filter)	120mm.	21	1.6
Hallmark (Filter Hard Pack)	100mm.	23	1.8

If your brand is not listed on these pages, check the FTC Cigarette Ratings in the back of the book.

4

PHASE II

"People in distress will sometimes prefer a problem that is familiar to a solution that is not."

N. Y. Times Magazine

The vast majority of smokers use brands in this Phase II category, with tar ratings between 14 and 19 mg. Although all come with filters, no smoker should deceive himself that these are "safe" cigarettes. They are not safe. They deliver an enormous amount of both nicotine and tar.

Even if you are now smoking the lowest brand in this group, 14 mg. tar and 1.0 mg. nicotine, you will have lowered both your tar and nicotine intake by 90% or more when you complete Phase V. If you follow through Phase VI, your total reduction from the Phase II level will be 90% or better.

The single greatest cause for failure throughout this plan is The Fumer Fallacy. You may very likely recall that on some occasion in recent years you failed to achieve a lower tar and nicotine level. The reason: you assumed that this unsatisfying new milder cigarette would be permanently unsatisfactory. Remember, by reducing your tar and nicotine level gradually, step by step, you will adjust quickly and with minimum discomfort. The goal, 90% reduction, is very much worth it.

You may recall W.C. Fields describing a town that ran out of gin: "We lived for days on nothing but food and water." This smoking plan does not require you to live without cigarettes; it does suggest that by paying careful attention to the rules in Chapter II you can easily adapt to this slightly reduced tar level and those that follow.

PHASE II
NON-MENTHOL
KING SIZE SOFT PACK FILTER

	Mg. Tar	*Mg. Nicotine*
Kool Naturals	14	1.0
Raleigh Lights	14	1.0
Viceroy Extra Mild	14	1.0
Galaxy	15	0.9
Viceroy	16	1.0
Vanguard	16	1.0
Raleigh Filter	16	1.1
Tareyton Filter	17	1.2
Marlboro	17	1.0
Lark	18	1.1
Pall Mall Filter	18	1.2
Old Gold Filter	18	1.2
Camel Filter	18	1.2
L & M	18	1.1
Eagle 20's	18	1.1
Winston	19	1.2
Chesterfield Filter	19	1.1

PHASE II
MENTHOL
KING SIZE SOFT PACK FILTER

	Mg. Tar	*Mg. Nicotine*
Vanguard	13	0.9
Marlboro	14	0.8
Alpine	14	0.8
Kool Milds	14	0.9
Belair	15	1.0
Kool	17	1.3
Newport	17	1.2
Montclair	18	1.3
Salem	18	1.2
Eagle 20's	18	1.1
Oasis	19	1.1

If your brand is not listed on these pages, check the FTC Cigarette Listings in the back of the book.

5

PHASE III

"People who give up smoking usually substitute something for it — like bragging."

The Better Way

Cigarette manufacturers continue to worry about the increased flow of research material painting an ever more deadly picture for the cigarette smoker. As a matter of fact, cigarette smoking causes about as many premature deaths in the United States as caused by infections, motor vehicles, suicides, homicides and diabetes combined.

Alarmed by the public's growing awareness that cigarettes are killing hundreds of thousands of Americans prematurely every year, the tobacco merchants have quite suddenly launched a flotilla of low-tar brands. This includes some established brands which have had their tar and nicotine levels drastically reduced. The number of brands in Phase III has tripled in recent years.

This is good news for the reader of THE SECOND-BEST SMOKING PLAN. A few years ago, there were only a few brands to choose from. Now there is something for everyone. Significantly, these new brands tend to have an even lower tar and nicotine content. It is anticipated that by the time you are reading this book there may be several more brands in this category.

Before making your move to a lower tar and nicotine level, it might be wise to review The Fumer Fallacy and Rules Are Tools.

PHASE III
NON-MENTHOL
KING SIZE SOFT PACK FILTER

	Mg. Tar	Mg. Nicotine
Tempo	7	0.5
Kent Golden Lights	8	0.6
L & M Lights	8	0.6
Merit	8	0.6
Tareyton Lights*	8	0.7
Fact*	8	0.7
Lucky Ten	9	0.6
Real*	9	0.8
Parliament	10	0.6
Vello	10	0.7
Vantage	11	0.7
Marlboro Lights	12	0.7
Doral	12	0.8
Multifilter	12	0.8
Winston Lights	12	0.9
Kent Kings*	12	1.0
Old Gold Lights*	12	1.0

*Appeared on the market too late for FTC Test Report dated June 1977.

PHASE III
MENTHOL
KING SIZE SOFT PACK FILTER

	Mg. Tar	Mg. Nicotine
Merit	8	0.5
Kent Golden Lights	8	0.7
Fact*	8	0.7
Kool Super Lights*	9	0.8
Newport Lights*	9	0.8
Real*	9	0.8
Vello	10	0.7
Multifilter	11	0.7
Vantage	11	0.8
Salem Lights	11	0.8
Doral	11	0.8

*Appeared on the market too late for FTC Test Report dated June 1977.

If your brand is not listed on these pages, check the FTC Cigarette Ratings in the back of the book.

6
PHASE IV

"When you have to make a choice and don't make it, that is in itself a choice."

William James

Everything you have read so far in this book is intended to answer your questions, dispel your doubts and stimulate you to change your smoking habits. The following suggestion from *The Shape of a Year*, by Jean Hersey (Scribner) is worth pondering and adapting to your routine as you move into Phases IV, V and VI.

"There is a wonderful way to develop the ability to adapt to change. It is a simple drill with a far-reaching effect: do something new and different once each day for a while. Not necessarily anything extremely unusual or startling — it can be merely doing a familiar thing in a different way. If you always put on your left shoe first, try putting on the right one. Walk down a different side of the street from the one you are used to.

"This, a psychologist friend told us, forms new pathways in the brain. Then, when next you meet a block in some direction of thinking or action, you will be able to accept it constructively or come up with a way around it which previously might have seemed to lead to a dead end.

"Entirely apart from developing the ability to adapt, this discipline is also rewarding and pleasant in the doing and in the new doors that it opens."

Perhaps the above will help you to "develop the ability to adapt." That, of course, is what THE SECOND-BEST SMOKING PLAN is all about. Check the brands in this Phase and then test, invest and adapt to this next lower tar and nicotine level.

PHASE IV
NON-MENTHOL
KING SIZE FILTER

	Mg. Tar	Mg. Nicotine
Decade*	5	0.5
True	5	0.4
Pall Mall Extra Mild*	6	0.5

* Appeared on the market too late for FTC Test Report dated June 1977.

PHASE IV
MENTHOL
KING SIZE FILTER

	Mg. Tar	Mg. Nicotine
Decade*	5	0.5
True	5	0.4

* Appeared on the market too late for FTC Test Report dated June 1977.

7
PHASE V

"I kissed my first woman and smoked my first cigarette on the same day," the great Toscanini is reputed to have said. "I have never had time for tobacco since."

We assume that most men, unlike Toscanini, have time for both and would prefer to love each of them well and wisely.

For the first time in the history of cigarettes, there are now two excellent brands on the market at the 1 mg tar, 0.1 mg.nicotine level. There will be others because this is where the future lies for the manufacturers and for the smokers. It seems evident that you choose to be among the first rather than the last to take advantage of this new cigarette category since you are concerned and intelligent enough to be involved in THE SECOND-BEST SMOKING PLAN.

In an excellent article on cigarettes in the May 1976 issue of *Consumer Reports,* there appeared the following paragraph which should help strengthen your resolve.

"If smokers were able to switch to such cigarettes, which are very low in tar, they would definitely reduce both their tar and nicotine intake. Moreover, when very-low-nicotine cigarettes have been tested for carbon monoxide yield, they have also ranked low in that substance. Carbon monoxide reduces the oxygen-carrying capacity of the blood, and the levels inhaled in cigarette smoke can place added stress on the heart and circulatory system. Thus, switching to a very-low-nicotine cigarette affords a three-way advantage to those who can tolerate them."

Every smoker can learn to tolerate and enjoy the mildest of cigarettes if he follows the instructions in this book.

PHASE V
NON-MENTHOL
KING SIZE FILTER

	Mg. Tar	*Mg. Nicotine*
Carlton	1	0.1
Now	1	0.1

PHASE V
MENTHOL
KING SIZE FILTER

	Mg. Tar	*Mg. Nicotine*
Carlton	1	0.1
Now	1	0.1

8
PHASE VI
THE HAPPY HOOKAH

"When you flee temptation, be sure you don't leave a forwarding address."

The Irish Digest

There is one more move you can make which will reduce your tar and nicotine intake to a minimum while you still enjoy the same amount of smoking per day. I am referring to a unique invention called the Aquafilter which is available at most major cigarette counters. This filter is based on the theory that tar and nicotine are soluble in water, and the Aquafilter employs a special cotton substance which is water-moistened. It functions very much like the original hookah.

Although there are other types of cigarette filters on the market, the water filter appears to be one of the best. As a matter of fact, some years ago a leading consumer-testing organization reported that the Aquafilter removed better than 50% of cigarette tars. Previous to that report, a mass consumer magazine had published their own test results which showed that the Aquafilter removed between 50% and 60% of both tar and nicotine.

The Aquafilter also has another useful advantage. Most cigarette filters have a permanent holder into which you insert a clean filter from time to time. If you have ever used one of these, you know how quickly some holders become gummed up, much like a pipe. The Aquafilter is a small, inconspicuous plastic unit which is disposable. Each filter is good for at least one package of cigarettes. They come in packages of ten.

Once again, you should go through the process of getting acclimated to a milder smoke. Invest in at least 30 filters and use them consistently. It is helpful to check the instructions on the back of the Aquafilter package. Although these filters are premoistened, if you should find a dry one, simply add a little water from the faucet and then blow out the excess moisture. Your first few days with the Aquafilter are going to be moderately difficult because the smoke is, once again, much milder. This water filter also seems to give you a cooler smoke which most users find a pleasant improvement. By the end of two or three weeks, you should be enjoying your smoking just as much as you ever did. If your original cigarette was a Winston or an even stronger brand, you will now have reduced your intake of tar and nicotine by more than 95%. *This means the amount of smoking you do in a full week involves far less tar and nicotine than you were taking in previously during a single day.*

PART II

ON THE SUBJECT OF QUITTING

"The 30-day smoking plan has become very popular — that's the one people decide they'll start on in about 30 days."
              Apologies to *Hugh Allen, Knoxville News-Sentinel*

1
SMOKER'S SELF-TESTING KIT

This effective and revealing self-testing kit for cigarette smokers was developed by Daniel Horn, Ph.D., director of the National Clearinghouse for Smoking and Health of the Public Health Service, and members of the Clearinghouse staff. We greatly appreciate their permission to include the test as an important part of this section on quitting.

SMOKER'S SELF-TESTING KIT

There are 4 short tests in this chapter to help you find out what you *know* about cigarette smoking and how you *feel* about it. They can tell you:
1. Whether you *really* want to quit smoking.
2. What you know about the effects of smoking on health.
3. What kind of smoker you are (*why* you smoke).
4. Whether the world you live in will help or hinder you if you do try to stop.

We believe that if you take a good hard look at the facts and that if you analyze your real feelings you may decide to quit smoking. Tests 1 and 2 are designed to help you take this look at yourself.

Tests 3 and 4 will give you some insight into what kind of smoker you are, and will reveal some of the problems you may run into when you try to quit.

The purpose of the tests is to develop your insight ... to help you understand your smoking habit and to help you decide what you want to do about it.

After you have taken each test, you will go on to an explanation of what your score means. Make sure, before reading this explanation, that you have answered each question and totaled your score. *Then* go on to the interpretation of your score.

TEST 1
DO YOU WANT TO CHANGE YOUR SMOKING HABITS?

For each statement, circle the number that most accurately indicates how you feel. For example, if you completely agree with the statement, circle 4, if you agree somewhat, circle 3, etc.

Important: Answer every question.

	completely agree	somewhat agree	somewhat disagree	completely disagree
A. Cigarette smoking might give me a serious illness.	4	3	2	1
B. My cigarette smoking sets a bad example for others.	4	2	2	1
C. I find cigarette smoking to be a messy kind of habit.	4	3	2	1
D. Controlling my cigarette smoking is a challenge to me.	4	3	2	1
E. Smoking causes shortness of breath.	4	3	2	1
F. If I quit smoking cigarettes it might influence others to stop.	4	3	2	1
G. Cigarettes cause damage to clothing and other personal property.	4	3	2	1
H. Quitting smoking would show that I have willpower.	4	3	2	1
I. My cigarette smoking will have a harmful effect on my health.	4	3	2	1
J. My cigarette smoking influences others close to me to take up or continue smoking.	4	3	2	1
K. If I quit smoking, my sense of taste or smell would improve.	4	3	2	1
L. I do not like the idea of feeling dependent on smoking.	4	3	2	1

HOW TO SCORE:
1. Enter the numbers you have circled to the Test 1 questions in the spaces below, putting the number you have circled to Question A over line A, to Question B over line B. etc.

2. Total the scores across on each line to get your totals. For example, the sum of your scores over lines A, E, and I gives you your score on *Health* — lines B, F, and J give the score on *Example*, etc.

					Totals
____	+	____	+	____	= ____
A		E		I	Health
____	+	____	+	____	= ____
B		F		J	Example
____	+	____	+	____	= ____
C		G		K	Esthetics
____	+	____	+	____	= ____
D		H		L	Mastery

Scores can vary from 3 to 12. Any score 9 and above is *high*; any score 6 and below is *low*.

SCORING TEST 1
Do You Want to Change Your Smoking Habits?

Why do you want to quit smoking? Are your reasons strong enough for you to make the effort to quit? Do you have enough reasons? This is something only you can decide.

Four common reasons for wanting to quit smoking cigarettes are: concern over the effects on *health*; desire to set an *example* for others; recognition of the unpleasant aspects (the *esthetics*) of smoking; and desire to exercise *self-control*.

Test 1 of the Smoker's Self-Testing Kit was designed to measure the importance of each of these reasons to you. The higher you score on any category, say *health*, the more important that reason is to you. A score of 9 or above in one of these categories indicates that this is one of the most important reasons why you may want to quit.

1. HEALTH

Research during the past 10 or 15 years has shown that cigarette smoking can be harmful to health. Knowing this, many people have recently stopped smoking and many others are considering it. If your score on the *health* factor is 9 or above, the health hazards of smoking may be enough to make you want to quit now.

If your score on this factor is low (6 or less), look at your scores on Test 2. They tell how much you know about the health hazard. You may be lacking important information or may even have incorrect information. If so, health considerations are not playing the important role they should in your decision to keep on smoking or to quit.

2. EXAMPLE

Some people stop smoking because they want to set a good example for others. Parents do it to make it easier for their children to resist starting to smoke; doctors do it to influence their patients; teachers want to help their students; sports stars want to set an example for their young fans; husbands want to influence their wives, and vice versa.

Such examples are an important influence on our behavior. Research shows that almost twice as many high school students smoke if both parents are smokers compared to those whose parents are non-smokers or former smokers.

If your score is low (6 or less), it may mean that you are not interested in giving up smoking in order to set an example for others. Perhaps you do not appreciate how important your example could be.

3. ESTHETICS (the unpleasant aspects)

People who score high, that is, 9 or above, in this category, recognize and are disturbed by some of the unpleasant aspects of smoking. The smell of stale smoke on their clothing, bad breath, and stains on their fingers and teeth might be reason enough to consider breaking the habit.

4. MASTERY (self-control)

If you score 9 or above on this factor, you are bothered by the knowledge that you cannot control your desire to smoke. You are not your own master. Awareness of this challenge to your self-control may make you want to quit.

Summary of Test 1

Test 1 has measured your attitude toward four of the most common reasons why people want to quit smoking. Consider those that are important to you. Even if none are important, you still may have a highly personal reason for wanting to change your habit. All in all, you may now see that you have reasons enough to want to quit smoking.

If you are still not sure, study the interpretation of your scores on Test 2 (the next test) to determine what you know about the effects of smoking on your health and what part that knowledge may play in your decision.

TEST 2
WHAT DO YOU THINK THE EFFECTS OF SMOKING ARE?

For each statement, circle the number that shows how you feel about it. Do you strongly agree, mildly agree, mildly disagree, or strongly disagree?
Important: Answer every question.

	strongly agree	mildly agree	mildly disagree	strongly disagree
A. Cigarette smoking is not nearly as dangerous as many other health hazards.	1	2	3	4
B. I don't smoke enough to get any of the diseases that cigarette smoking is supposed to cause.	1	2	3	4
C. If a person has already smoked for many years, it probably won't do him much good to stop.	1	2	3	4
D. It would be hard for me to give up smoking cigarettes.	1	2	3	4
E. Cigarette smoking is enough of a health hazard for something to be done about it.	4	3	2	1
F. The kind of cigarette I smoke is much less likely than other kinds to give me any of the diseases that smoking is supposed to cause.	1	2	3	4
G. As soon as a person quits smoking cigarettes he begins to recover from much of the damage that smoking has caused.	4	3	2	1
H. It would be hard for me to cut down to half the number of cigarettes I now smoke.	1	2	3	4
I. The whole problem of cigarette smoking and health is a very minor one.	1	2	3	4
J. I haven't smoked long enough to worry about the diseases that cigarette smoking is supposed to cause.	1	2	3	4
K. Quitting smoking helps a person to live longer.	4	3	2	1

L. It would be difficult for me to make any substantial change in my smoking habits.	1	2	3	4

HOW TO SCORE:
1. Enter the number you have circled in the Test 2 questions in the spaces below, putting the number you have circled to Question A over line A, to Question B over line B, etc.
2. Total the 3 scores across on each line to get your totals. For example, the sum of your scores over lines A, E, and I gives you your score on *Importance* — lines B, F, and J give the score on *Personal Relevance*, etc.

                 Totals

_____ + _____ + _____ = _____
 A   E   I   **Importance**

_____ + _____ + _____ = _____
 B   F   J   **Personal Relevance**

_____ + _____ + _____ = _____
 C   G   K   **Value of Stopping**

_____ + _____ + _____ = _____
 D   H   L   **Capability for Stopping**

Scores can vary from 3 to 12. Any score 9 and above is *high*; any score 6 and below is *low*.

SCORING TEST 2.
What Do You Think the Effects of Smoking Are?

To attempt to give up smoking you must do more than simply acknowledge that "cigarette smoking may be harmful to your health." You must be aware that smoking is an *important* problem, that it has *personal* meaning for you, that there is *value* to be gained from stopping, and that people are *capable* of stopping. Test 2 measures the strength of your recognition of each of these factors.

If your score is 9 or above on any factor, that factor supports your desire to try to stop smoking. If your score is 6 or below, that factor will not help you, but note that you may have scored low because you lack correct information. For every factor for which you *do* have a low score, read the accompanying explanatory material with special care.

1. IMPORTANCE

Cancer, heart disease, respiratory diseases — all related to smoking — are among the most serious to which man is exposed. You should not shrug off the growing evidence that they cause death and severe disability. Yet you may be doing this if your score is 6 or lower on the first part of Test 2.

Research has shown that one death in every three is an "extra" death among men who die between the ages of 35 and 60, because cigarette smokers have higher death rates than nonsmokers. 1 day of every 5 lost from work because of illness, 1 day in every 10 spent in bed because of illness, 1 day of every 8 days of restricted activity — all are "extra," because cigarette smokers suffer more disability than non-smokers.

2. PERSONAL RELEVANCE

Some smokers kid themselves into thinking: "It can't happen to me — only to the other guy." If you score 6 or below, you may be one of these people.

Your reasoning may go something like this: "I don't really smoke enough to be hurt by it. It takes two packs a day over a period of many years before harmful effects show up."

Unfortunately, this is not true. Even people who smoke less than half a pack a day show significantly higher death rates than nonsmokers. Breathing capacity can diminish after only a very few years of regular smoking. Even what used to be considered light smoking, such as half a pack a day, can be harmful.

3. VALUE OF STOPPING

Evidence shows that there are benefits to health when you give up smoking — even if you have smoked for many years. A score of 6 or lower indicates that you do not realize this.

There are real advantages in giving up smoking even for long-term smokers; people who quit before any symptoms of illness or impairment occur suffer lower death rates than those who continue to smoke, and reduce the likelihood of serious illness.

People who have had heart attacks and those with stomach ulcers and chronic respiratory diseases should definitely give up smoking. It is difficult if not impossible to control such illnesses if they do not.

4. CAPABILITY FOR STOPPING

If your score is 6 or lower on this part of the test, you believe that it will be hard for you to quit. But you may find encouragement in the fact that over 20 million adults are now successful ex-smokers. Of these, over 100,000 doctors, well over half of those who were ever cigarette smokers, have successfully quit.

In the following test, No. 3, you will gain some insight into the reasons why you smoke. With this new knowledge, it may be easier for you to give up smoking than you thought it would be. At any rate, you must develop confidence that it is possible for you to control your smoking; if you do not, you are less likely to succeed in your attempt to quit.

Summary of Test 2

Review your scores on the four factors that this test measures. For those on which you scored in the *middle* or *low* brackets, study the explanatory material. If this pamphlet does not answer all your questions, you may get additional material from the Public Health Service, your local health department, and such agencies as the National Tuberculosis and Respiratory Disease Association, American Cancer Society, American Heart Association, or you public library.

Now, you should be ready to decide whether or not you are going to try to give up smoking. If you have strong enough reasons to do so, if you know enough about the real effects of smoking, if you have not been led astray by misinformation, and if you will not try to fool yourself, you are ready.

TEST 3
WHY DO YOU SMOKE?

Here are some statements made by people to describe what they get out of smoking cigarettes. How *often* do you feel this way when smoking them? Circle one number for each statement.

Important: Answer every question

	always	frequently	occasionally	seldom	never
A. I smoke cigarettes in order to keep myself from slowing down.	5	4	3	(2)	1
B. Handling a cigarette is part of the enjoyment of smoking it.	(5)	4	3	2	1
C. Smoking cigarettes is pleasant and relaxing.	5	(4)	3	2	1
D. I light up a cigarette when I feel angry about something.	(5)	4	3	2	1
E. When I have run out of cigarettes I find it almost unbearable until I can get them.	(5)	4	3	2	1
F. I smoke cigarettes automatically without even being aware of it.	5	4	(3)	2	1
G. I smoke cigarettes to stimulate me, to perk myself up.	5	4	3	(2)	1
H. Part of the enjoyment of smoking a cigarette comes from the steps I take to light up.	(5)	4	3	2	1
I. I find cigarettes pleasurable.	5	(4)	3	2	1
J. When I feel uncomfortable or upset about something, I light up a cigarette.	(5)	4	3	2	1
K. I am very much aware of the fact when I am not smoking a cigarette.	5	(4)	3	2	1

L. I light up a cigarette without realizing I still have one burning in the ashtray.	5	4	3	(2)	1
M. I smoke cigarettes to give me a "lift."	5	4	3	(2)	1
N. When I smoke a cigarette, part of the enjoyment is watching the smoke as I exhale it.	(5)	4	3	2	1
O. I want a cigarette most when I am comfortable and relaxed.	(5)	4	3	2	1
P. When I feel "blue" or want to take my mind off cares and worries, I smoke cigarettes.	5	4	3	(2)	1
Q. I get a real gnawing hunger for a cigarette when I haven't smoked for a while.	(5)	4	3	2	1
R. I've found a cigarette in my mouth and didn't remember putting it there.	5	4	3	(2)	1

HOW TO SCORE:

1. Enter the numbers you have circled to the Test 3 questions in the spaces below, putting the number you have circled to Question A over line A, to Question B over line B, etc.
2. Total the 3 scores on each line to get your totals. For example, the sum of your scores over lines A, G, and M gives you your score on *Stimulation* — lines B, H, and N give the score on *Handling*, etc.

				Totals
2	2	2	=	
A	G	M		Stimulation
5	5	5	=	
B	H	N		Handling
4	4	5	=	
C	I	O		Pleasurable Relaxation
5	5	2	=	
D	J	P		Crutch: Tension Reduction
5	4	5	=	
E	K	Q		Craving: Psychological Addiction
3	2	2	=	
F	L	R		Habit

Scores can vary from 3 to 15. Any score 11 and above is *high*; any score 7 and below is *low*.

SCORING TEST 3.
Why Do You Smoke?

What kind of smoker are you? What do you get out of smoking? What does it do for you? This test is designed to provide you with a score on each of 6 factors which describe many people's smoking. Your smoking may be well characterized by only one of these factors, or by a combination of factors. In any event, this test will help you identify what you use smoking for and what kind of satisfaction you think you get from smoking.

The six factors measured by this test describe one or another way of experiencing or managing certain kinds of feelings. Three of these feeling-states represent the *positive* feelings people get from smoking: (1) a sense of increased energy or *stimulation*, (2) the satisfaction of *handling* or manipulating things, and (3) the enhancing of *pleasurable feelings* accompanying a state of well-being. The fourth is the *decreasing of negative feelings* by reducing a state of tension or feelings of anxiety, anger, shame, etc. The fifth is a complex pattern of increasing and decreasing "craving" for a cigarette representing a psychological *addiction* to cigarettes. The sixth is *habit* smoking which takes place in an absence of feeling — purely automatic smoking.

A score of 11 or above on any factor indicates that this factor is an important source of satisfaction for you. The higher your score (15 is the highest), the more important a particular factor is in your smoking and the more useful the discussion of that factor can be in your attempt to quit.

A few words of warning: If you give up smoking, you may have to learn to get along without the satisfactions that smoking gives you. Either that, or you will have to find some more acceptable way of getting this satisfaction. In either case, you need to know just what it is you get out of smoking before you can decide whether to forego the satisfactions it gives you or to find another way to achieve them.

1. STIMULATION

If you score high or fairly high on this factor, it means that you are one of those smokers who is stimulated by the cigarette — you feel that it helps wake you up, organize your energies, and keep you going. If you try to give up smoking, you may want a safe substitute, *a brisk walk* or moderate exercise, for example, whenever you feel the urge to smoke.

2. HANDLING

Handling things can be satisfying, but there are many ways to keep your hands busy without lighting up or playing with a cigarette. Why not toy with a pen or pencil? Or try doodling. Or play with a coin, a piece of jewelry, or some other harmless object.

There are plastic cigarettes to play with, or you might even use a real cigarette if you can trust yourself not to light it.

3. ACCENTUATION OF PLEASURE — PLEASURABLE RELAXATION

It is not always easy to find out whether you use the cigarette to feel *good*, that is, get real, honest pleasure out of smoking (Factor 3) or to keep from feeling so *bad* (Factor 4). About two-thirds of smokers score high or fairly high on *accentuation of pleasure*, and about half of those also score as high or higher on *reduction of negative feelings*.

Those who do get real pleasure out of smoking often find that an honest consideration of the harmful effects of their habit is enough to help them quit. They substitute eating, drinking, social activities, and physical activities — within reasonable bounds — and find they do not seriously miss their cigarettes.

4. REDUCTION OF NEGATIVE FEELINGS, OR "CRUTCH"

Many smokers use the cigarette as a kind of crutch in moments of stress or discomfort, and on occasion it may work; the cigarette is sometimes used as a tranquilizer. But the heavy smoker, the person who tries to handle severe personal problems by smoking many times a day, is apt to discover that cigarettes do not help him deal with his problems effectively.

When it comes to quitting, this kind of smoker may find it easy to stop when everything is going well, but may be tempted to start again in a time of crisis. Again, physical exertion, eating, drinking, or social activity — in moderation — may serve as useful substitutes for cigarettes, even in times of tension. The choice of a substitute depends on what will achieve the same effect with having any appreciable risk.

5. "CRAVING" OR PSYCHOLOGICAL ADDICTION

Quitting smoking is difficult for the person who scores high on this factor, that of *psychological addiction*. For him, the craving for the next cigarette begins to build up the moment he puts one out, so tapering off is not likely to work. He must go "cold turkey."

It may be helpful for him to smoke more than usual for a day or two, so that the taste for cigarettes is spoiled, and then isolate himself completely from cigarettes until the craving is gone. Giving up cigarettes may be so difficult and cause so much discomfort that once he does quit, he will find it easy to resist the temptation to go back to smoking because he knows that some day he will have to go through the same agony again.

6. HABIT

This kind of smoker is no longer getting much satisfaction from his cigarettes. He just lights them frequently without even realizing he is doing so. He may find it easy to quit and stay off if he can break the habit patterns he has built up. Cutting down gradually may be quite effective if there is a change in the way the cigarettes are smoked and the conditions under which they are smoked. The key to success is becoming *aware* of each cigarette you smoke. This can be done by asking yourself, "Do I really want this cigarette?" You may be surprised at how many you do not want.

Summary of Test 3

If you do not score high on any of the six factors, chances are that you do not smoke very much or have not been smoking for very many years. If so, giving up smoking — and staying off — should be easy.

If you score high on several categories, you apparently get several kinds of satisfaction from smoking and will have to find several solutions. Certain combinations of scores may indicate that giving up smoking will be especially difficult. Those who score high on both Factor 4 and Factor 5, *reduction of negative feelings* and *craving*, may have a particularly hard time in going off smoking and in staying off. However, there are ways to do it; many smokers represented by this combination have been able to quit.

Others who score high on Factors 4 and 5 may find it useful to change their patterns of smoking and cut down at the same time. They can try to smoke fewer cigarettes, smoke them only half-way down, use low-tar-and-nicotine cigarettes, and inhale less often and less deeply. After several months of this temporary solution, they may find it easier to stop completely.

You must make two important decisions: (1) whether to try to do without the satisfactions you get from smoking or find an appropriate, less hazardous substitute, and (2) whether to try to cut out cigarettes all at once, or taper off.

Your scores should guide you in making both of these decisions.

TEST 4
DOES THE WORLD AROUND YOU MAKE IT EASIER OR HARDER TO CHANGE YOUR SMOKING HABITS?

Indicate by circling the appropriate numbers whether you feel the following statements are true or false.

Important: Answer every question.

	true or mostly true	false or mostly false
A. Doctors have decreased or stopped their smoking of cigarettes in the past 10 years.	2	1
B. In recent years there seem to be more rules about where you are allowed to smoke.	2	1
C. Cigarette advertising makes smoking appear attractive to me.	1	2
D. Schools are trying to discourage children from smoking.	2	1
E. Doctors are trying to get their patients to stop smoking.	2	1
F. Someone has recently tried to persuade me to cut down or quit smoking cigarettes.	2	1
G. The constant repetition of cigarette advertising makes it hard for me to quit smoking.	1	2
H. Both government and private health organizations are actively trying to discourage people from smoking.	2	1
I. A doctor has, at least once, talked to me about my smoking.	2	1
J. It seems as though an increasing number of people object to having someone smoke near them.	2	1
K. Some cigarette advertisements make me feel like smoking.	1	2
L. Congressmen and other legislators are showing concern with smoking and health.	2	1

M. The people around you, particularly those who are close to you (e.g., relatives, friends, office associates), may make it easier or more difficult for you to give up smoking by what they say or do. What about these people? Would you say that they make giving up smoking or staying off cigarettes more difficult for you than it would be otherwise? (Circle the number to the left of the statement that best describes your situation.)
   3 They make it much more difficult than it would be otherwise.
   4 They make it somewhat more difficult than it would be otherwise.
   5 They make it somewhat easier than it would be otherwise.
   6 They make it much easier than it would be otherwise.

HOW TO SCORE:
1. Enter the numbers you have circled on the Test 4 questions in the spaces below, putting the number you have circled to Question A over line A, to Question B over line B, etc.
2. Total the 3 scores across on each line to get your totals. For example, the sum of your scores over lines A, E, and I gives you your score on *Doctors* — lines B, F, and J give the score on *General Climate*, etc.

					Totals	
___A___	+	___E___	+	___I___	=	_____ Doctors
___B___	+	___F___	+	___J___	=	_____ General Climate
___C___	+	___G___	+	___K___	=	_____ Advertising Influence
___D___	+	___H___	+	___L___	=	_____ Key Group Influences
				___M___	=	_____ Interpersonal Influences

Scores can vary from 3 to 6: 6 is *high*; 5, high middle; 4, low middle; 3, *low*.

SCORING TEST 4.
Does The World Around You Make it Easier or Harder to Change Your Smoking Habit?

What will happen when you try to quit smoking? Aside from the problems that may arise within yourself because of the strength of the smoking habit and what you get out of it, to what extent will you get help from what is happening around you?

This test will help you identify which of 5 factors may be of particular importance to you in providing support to your efforts to quit smoking. A factor on which your score is 5 or 6 represents a part of your environment that can be a help to you. A factor on which your score is 3 or 4 indicates a situation that may hurt your chances of staying off cigarettes.

1. DOCTORS

Many people are influenced by what their physicians do and say about the smoking problem. We know that the overwhelming majority of doctors accept cigarette smoking as a serious health hazard and that well over half of the doctors who used to smoke have given it up. If you score 5 or 6 on this factor, talk to your doctor about smoking and get his support.

2. GENERAL CLIMATE

A score of 3 or 4 on this factor indicates that the environment in which you live and work will not be very helpful in your effort to quit smoking. You may need to seek a more congenial environment. If so, make a point of talking to or associating with people who are trying to stop smoking or who have succeeded in doing so. Also, avoid places where smoking is permitted in favor of places where smoking is prohibited.

3. ADVERTISING INFLUENCE

A score of 3 or 4 on this factor indicates that you are strongly influenced by cigarette advertising. You may have to avoid exposing yourself to these influences until you can withstand them.

4. KEY GROUP INFLUENCES

Knowing the position taken by certain "key groups" can be very important for some people, and a score of 5 or 6 on this factor indicates that you are aware of the influence of such groups. Some people are strongly influenced by the actions of the federal government, some by public and private health agencies, others by schools. All these are on public record that smoking is harmful and all are engaged in programs to reduce cigarette smoking.

5. INTERPERSONAL INFLUENCES

For most of us there are certain people who are particularly important to us. What these people think, do, and say can make a big difference in the way we behave. For some it is a husband or a wife. For others it is their children or their parents. For still others it is the people at work. Because there are so many possible influences, it is difficult to determine which ones are important to you through a simple set of questions. Your answer to

Question M should serve as a guide in this area. If your score is 5 or 6, the people who are important to you are likely to be helpful in your effort to quit smoking. If, however, your score is 3 or 4, these important people may not be helpful unless you actively seek their support.

Summary of Test 4

Your chances of staying off cigarettes permanently depend to a large extent on the support you get from the world around you. Your scores on this test identify the "helps" and "hindrances" in your own environment. With this knowledge, you may be able to find ways to improve your chances.

2
TRICK OR TRACHEA

"Does the smoker know you're out, Ce Cilia?
Does he know what you're about, Ce Cilia?"

    The smoker's ritual morning cough is one of the most irritating yet least understood of his various aggravations. The unpleasantness is a shared experience whether you are the innocent bystander and must listen to this uncontrollable throat-clearing storm, or you are the hacker and for some mysterious reason seem destined each morning to a spasm of coughing until your throat is reasonably clear. The smoker realizes very well that cigarettes are the cause. But it is a rare victim indeed who understands or perhaps even wants to understand why the act of drawing clouds of tar and nicotine into his lungs two or three hundred times a day produces these diurnal convulsions.

    It is fortunate for the cigarette peddlers that this rather unlovely daily performance does not usually afflict the cigarette smoker until some years after he first starts smoking. If teenagers could get right into this awake, arise and cough routine, it might make the whole smoking and peer group pressure scene that

BROOM-HILDA

By permission of Chicago Tribune-New York News Syndicate.

much less attractive. Let us not forget that 1,000,000 young people alive today will die of lung cancer caused by smoking.

Smoker's cough does take some years to develop because your cilia really don't want to take it (the smoke) lying down. They perform a vital function, and they keep on trying until they are totally destroyed. In "Tobacco and Your Health" by Dr. Harold S. Diehl, (McGraw-Hill Book Co., 1969), their function is described as follows: "The bronchial tubes of the lungs have a remarkable protective mechanism. The cells lining these tubes and tubules secrete mucus, a sticky fluid which collects particles of soot, dust and other substances in inhaled air. This mucus is carried up through the bronchial tubes and the trachea by the action of the cilia and is either swallowed or expectorated. These cilia are little hairlike structures which protrude from the inner surface of the respiratory passages and maintain a continuous whiplike motion of about 900 beats a minute. *Their movement causes mucus to flow up and out of the lungs.* Particles of inhaled dust and other substances trapped in the mucus are thus removed, keeping the lungs clean and protecting the bronchial tubes from damage. If the pollution of the inhaled air is more than this system can remove, or if the cilia are destroyed or fail to work, this protection is lost. Cigarette smoke first slows, then stops ciliary action and eventually destroys the cilia, thereby exposing delicate membranes to injury by substances inhaled in cigarette smoke or in the air we breathe."

A smoker with a persistent cough may well be on his way to chronic bronchitis and quite possibly to the dreaded emphysema.

Now, wouldn't this be a proper time to make the big decision and select a day to quit?

3
A CIGAR OR PIPE WON'T MAKE IT RIGHT

"I make it a point never to smoke more than one cigar at a time."
Mark Twain

If the opportunity presents itself, take a moment to observe the pipe or cigar smoker. If you watch carefully, it is not difficult to determine whether or not he inhales the smoke. Most studies indicate that, while 90% of cigarette smokers report inhaling, only 30% of pipe smokers and 20% of cigar smokers admit to even slight inhalation. If your subject does inhale, it is tempting to ask, "When did you switch from cigarettes to a pipe (or cigar)?" And before he can answer, add, "Incidentally, do you inhale?" The reaction is fairly predictable. "I only inhale a little bit from time to time," and "How did you know I used to smoke cigarettes?"

The unfortunate fact is that medium to heavy cigarette smokers who switch to pipes or cigars almost invariably continue to inhale although they tend to be unaware of it. I have talked to pipe smokers who, while exhaling streams of tobacco smoke through their nostrils, insist that they rarely inhale any smoke. When I

Reprinted with permission of Ted Key. Copyright and world rights reserved by King Features Syndicate.

suggest that it is difficult to expel smoke through one's nose without first "swallowing" it, they are puzzled and even indignant.

It is probably true, however, that they do not inhale the smoke as deeply into the lungs as the average cigarette smoker, nor as frequently. Mortality rates from cancer of the oral cavity, larynx and esophagus are approximately equal in users of cigars, pipes *and* cigarettes. Inhalation is evidently not necessary to expose these sites to tobacco smoke.

Coronary heart disease, lung cancer, emphysema, chronic bronchitis are diseases which are clearly associated with cigarette smoking. For cigar and pipe smokers, these diseases occur only slightly more often than for non-smokers. In countries where smokers tend to use more cigars and inhale them to a greater degree, evidence shows that rates of lung cancer become elevated to levels approaching those of cigarette smokers.

Dr. Niel Solomon in the *Boston Globe*, answering a letter writer who had made the cigar substitution and felt rather righteous about it, responded as follows: "Having been a cigarette smoker, you're in a special problem category: Your long-time use of cigarettes is likely to have conditioned you to more or less automatic inhaling. If you've carried over this pattern and still inhale (which you may be doing unconsciously) you might just as well not have gone through all that tremendous agony you subjected yourself to. Inhaling the smoke of pipes or cigars may be even more dangerous than inhaling cigarette smoke."

The moral is obvious: If you are going to say farewell to cigarettes, don't strike up a new acquaintance with a tobacco tantalizer in a different dress.

4
AND NOW — SOMETHING SPECIAL FOR THE LADIES

> "My advice to girls:
> first, don't smoke — to excess;
> second, don't drink — to excess;
> third, don't marry — to excess."
>
> *Mark Twain*

If, over the centuries, a parade of chauvinistic men have established a less than equal world for women, it would now appear that the neuter cigarette dispenses its own list of injustices to the female of the species. And since these unique tobacco taboos are concerned exclusively with her reproductive system, it might rightfully inspire an indignant cry in pigeon French "Heave La Difference."

ITEM: THE PILL

It has been established that the effects of the pill and cigarette-smoking are synergistic, one boosting the adverse action of the other. University of Michigan

Pat Oliphant. Copyright 1978 The Washington Star. Reprinted with permission Los Angeles Times Syndicate.

sociologist, Anrudh Jain, in a study sponsored by The Population Council, has shown that the chances of death by heart attack or stroke skyrocket for those women who combine smoking and the pill. The use of either by itself increases the risk, but not to such an alarming degree. For example, women aged 40 to 44 who use the pill but do not smoke had an average death rate due to heart attack and stroke of only 7 per 100,000. This is only one-third the risk of death from pregnancy and childbirth for women that age. Pill users in this age group who smoked 15 or more cigarettes per day were found to face a mortality risk of 83 per 100,000, or about twelve times as great. Although the deaths per 100,000 are considerably lower for women aged 30 to 39, a similar relationship exists with the synergistic effects increasing the risk 4 to 5 times.

ITEM: MENOPAUSE

Women who smoke are likely to undergo menopause at a younger age than non-smokers, and the more a woman smokes, the earlier her menopause is likely to occur. This came to light in a study conducted by Drs. Hershel Jick and Jane Porter of the Boston University School of Medicine and Allan Morrison of the Harvard School of Public Health. The survey included more than 3,500 middle-aged women in 7 countries.

Women past menopause have been shown to have a higher rate of coronary heart disease than premenopausal women of the same age. But since smoking is known to increase a person's chances of developing heart disease, and has now been shown to accelerate the onset of menopause, smoking, rather than menopause itself, may be the real culprit in these heart disease statistics.

ITEM: PREGNANCY AND BIRTH

In an English study of 2,000 pregnant women, a significantly higher percentage of unsuccessful pregnancies (that is, abortion, stillbirth or neonatal death) occurred among women who smoked during pregnancy than among those who did not. Results indicated that 20% of the unsuccessful pregnancies in women who smoked regularly would have been successful if the women were non-smokers.

In a research project in the United States, an analysis of over 100,000 births shows that the infants of mothers who smoked during pregnancy have a mean birth weight of 6 ounces less than the infants born to non-smoking mothers. The reduction in birth weight is greater among heavy-smoking mothers than light-smoking mothers.

Linked to these discouraging statistics is a study done at the University of Washington which indicates that unexplained "crib deaths" strike with significantly greater frequency against infants whose mothers smoked during and after pregnancy.

A National Child Development study in London shows that at ages 7 and 11, children of mothers who smoked 10 or more cigarettes a day after the twentieth week of pregnancy are, on the average, 1 cm. shorter and 3-4 months behind on their reading and arithmetic attainments at school compared with the children of mothers who did not smoke after the twentieth week.

It appears that this particular sin of the mother (smoking) may indeed be passed on to her progeny. However, the male is not necessarily free of tobacco sin as regards his role in the birth process. An 8-year study by the German Research Society indicates that sperm may be damaged by heavy nicotine intake, accounting for the excessive number of stillbirths that occurred when the father was a heavy smoker.

Reprinted by permission of Newspaper Enterprise Association.

5

IS THERE SUCH A THING AS WILL POWER AND WHY IS MINE MISSING?

> "Though it may be convenient and intelligible to talk of a man having a strong Will or a good Memory, or a powerful Reason, it is generally agreed by psychologists today that this division of the personality into departments such as "Will", "Memory", "Reason", is erroneous and misleading and that these words cannot rightly be thought of as standing for real entities."
>
> *E. R. Emmet*
> *Handbook of Logic*

Most psychologists believe there is no such thing as will power. Of course, the dictionary does have a definition and describes will power as "control over one's impulses and actions." The question is, how does one capture and employ this elusive control?

Since, as a general rule, people are free to make their own personal decisions and control their own actions, they should be able to use their will power to accomplish such things as abstinence from fattening foods, alcohol or cigarettes. *Presto,* no fat people, no alcoholics, no cigarette fiends.

For most of us, it doesn't seem to function that easily. So where did all the will power go, or was it ever there?

Calling on your will power to help avoid food, alcohol or cigarettes means constantly battling temptation. The opportunity to eat, drink or smoke presents itself repeatedly during our waking hours. Each presentation demands that will power be called on to strengthen our resolve. Each confrontation produces another difficult struggle with our conscience and our good intentions.

In place of unreliable will power, we should employ *decision.* Let us examine how this might work for the dieter.

We want to lose 20 pounds which means we must diet. As we contemplate this unpleasant prospect, we begin to vacillate and reconsider. But we finally conclude that these 20 extra pounds of fat make us so uneasy and unhappy that they definitely must go.

Now, and only now, we make an unequivocal *decision* to lose 20 pounds.

We *decide* to eat no more than 1000 calories a day. We also *decide* that *all* alcoholic drinks are out for the duration.

We have not conferred with our will power as to whether it would back us up. We know better than that. Instead, we made a thoughtful, considered decision.

Three days into the diet, we arrive at a dinner party.

With the diet momentarily out of mind, we approach the bar with our usual happy anticipation. And then we remember. Damn it! We would really like to have a drink to launch us into the festivities.

If we were counting on our fickle will power for this emergency, all those familiar rationalizations would start bouncing around inside our head; i.e., we mustn't insult the host and one little drink won't do any harm. We'll drink soda instead of tonic with the gin to save calories. We will try to nurse only one or two drinks through the entire evening. And on it goes.

Fortunately, we don't have to go through any of these mental contortions. What's more, we won't sabotage the diet. You see, we made a firm decision, and there is nothing else to consider. The decision is fixed and eliminates entertaining any possible compromises.

When the host offers a drink, there is no temptation, no wavering, no pangs of self-denial. You request a tall glass of soda water with a dash of bitters or a squeeze of lime and are pleasantly surprised with its refreshing taste. You also move up a few notches in your own self image. And it didn't hurt a bit.

Indecision means constant, uncomfortable, tempting, uncertainty. A firm decision very nearly means the mission is as good as accomplished. When the moment arrives to quit smoking, forget will power and strive instead to make a carefully prepared decision.

In his excellent book, "You Can Quit Smoking in 14 Days," Walter S. Ross quotes a man from Quebec, Canada as follows: "I had been smoking for fourteen years. One Sunday night I was going out for cigarettes. My wife said she needed milk for the kids' breakfast. I didn't have enough money for both, and there was nowhere to cash a check late Sunday evening. The fact that I had to think about which to buy was, in my opinion, *sick*. I haven't had a smoke since."

This man obviously didn't consult with his will-o-the-wisp will power as to whether it would back him up. It wasn't even a question of "trying" to stop. "Trying" portends a gigantic never-ending struggle with your conscience.

The man suddenly recognized his situation in all its stark, ugly reality. Was buying milk for his children *less important* than his continuing to suck useless, poisonous, tar and gases into his lungs?

The man made a decision — a firm, irrevocable, no-loopholes decision. Once you have made *that* kind of decision, the act of quitting is nearly a *fait accompli*. Anything *less* than that is begging for trouble and unlikely to succeed. The slightest uncertainty on your part allows temptation to toy with you each time the excruciating desire to smoke presents itself. But if you *know* you are not going to smoke no matter what, those moments of intense desire pass more quickly and appear with less and less frequency.

Alvin R. Jaffin, Director of the American Health Foundation, puts it this way: "All we know is that some people *try* to quit. Others *quit*. Somehow, they are able to say to themselves, '*this is not a negotiable issue any more.*' It's like what happens on the subways: you don't smoke, and you don't die. But the minute you get to the steps, you're dying for a smoke. That's because smoking on subways is a non-negotiable issue."

6
NOW THAT YOU'RE COMFORTABLE
(with this low tar and nicotine level)
QUIT

"The worst boss anyone can have is a bad habit."

Monta Crane

At 50, will you be at the peak of your powers and ability to enjoy life, or will you be a quarter of a century older than necessary — age 50 going on 75?

Dr. Linus Pauling, twice a Nobel Prize winner, puts a most persuasive case for quitting as follows: "A one-pack-a-day smoker at the age of 50 is as old physiologically as a non-smoker aged 58. A two-pack-a-day smoker at 50 is as old as a non-smoker aged 66. A person who has smoked 3 packs a day is as old physiologically and has the same high incidence of disease as the average non-smoker at 74."

There is a special reason why THE SECOND-BEST SMOKING PLAN can help you to quit; to wit, nicotine is physiologically addicting. The less nicotine your cigarettes feed your system, the easier your system will adjust to getting along without it when you cease smoking.

In "Learning to Live Without Cigarettes," originally published by Doubleday in 1968, Allen, Angerman and Fackler describe what happens when you inhale cigarette smoke.

"When nicotine enters the blood stream, the heartbeat immediately accelerates, in some individuals up to 40%. This results in an increased blood flow, which can be measured by a rise in blood pressure. The increased flow of blood through the system speeds up the chemical processes of the body. More oxygen is delivered to the brain, and more energy is furnished to the body cells and organs. This energy, in the form of fuel sugars, has been released from the liver as a result of the simultaneous secretion of adrenalin into the blood stream. These fuel sugars, when burned by oxygen in the body cells, produce energy which normally is needed to live and work. In the smoker, though, they are needed to break down the toxic elements of the nicotine so that they can be quickly eliminated through the kidneys."

It is this increase in the flow of blood and all that follows which results in the feeling of "lift" that is experienced by the smoker when he inhales nicotine. Experiencing this lift becomes habitual and in time addictive.

The most popular brands deliver about 1.3 milligrams of nicotine per cigarette. When the average smoker quits cold, he or she may develop unpleasant physical withdrawal symptoms. This explains why it is so important to reduce your tar and nicotine levels slowly step by step. When you reach the mildest cigarette level, your nicotine intake has been reduced from 70% to 95%. The Aquafilter, if you choose to use it, will eliminate 50% of what little is left. By following THE SECOND-BEST SMOKING PLAN and acclimating yourself gradually to a lower tar and nicotine level, there should be only mild temporary discomfort when you stop smoking for good.

"Procrastination — A fault that most people put off trying to correct."

Indianapolis News

Let's get to the moment of truth when you thoughtfully and carefully make the decision to quit. This is an excellent time to gain reinforcement by reading one or more of the following books: the previously mentioned "Learning to Live Without Cigarettes" (Doubleday), "How To Stop Smoking" by Herbert Brean (Pocketbook), and "You Can Quit Smoking in 14 Days" by Walter S. Ross (Reader's Digest-Press).

Set a target date for quitting. If possible, choose a less hectic period when temptations to smoke will be minimized. Be mentally prepared. A week before quitting, start keeping a diary of every cigarette smoked. Attach a file card to the back of the package and record the time and place every time you light up. Start anticipating the joy of getting rid of the diary, the matches, the butts, the cough, the smelly clothes, the foul mouth, the poisons, the cigarette burns, the expense, the inconvenience, the monkey on your back, and perhaps most of all, the all-too-visible demeaning stupidity of smoking.

Prepare yourself for the most difficult moments, those times of day and those activities when a cigarette seems most fitting and enjoyable — with the first cup of coffee, after a good meal, with the first drink, after sex. Anticipate and make ready in advance for these crucial encounters. Avoid coffee and/or liquor completely for the first week, substitute water or fruit juice. This helps kill the association. After a meal, get up immediately and start another activity. Take a walk. The fresh air will taste better than it has in a long time.

During the first weeks, it sometimes helps to put yourself in a situation where smoking is forbidden: the library, the movies, a concert, the non-smoking areas in public places — subways.

During these first crucial days, there may occasionally be excruciating moments when a voice inside starts screaming: "The hell with it. Get some tar and nicotine in here." There follow some suggestions for getting through these dangerous moments and buttoning the lip of that persistent but steadily diminishing inner voice.

1. Take a deep breath, hold it, let it out slowly. Repeat 4 or 5 times. By relaxing tensions, desire for a cigarette is reduced and ultimately disappears.

2. Instead of succumbing to a cigarette, start to figure how much money you will be saving each month by not smoking. Multiply this by 12 and start a list of things you might want to buy with this new-found wealth. This gets your mind on to a different track and

an excellent maneuver for the tougher moments.

From a first-person article in *The Reader's Digest*: "An overwhelming desire for a cigarette is possibly sweeping over you right now. But why should a puny piece of paper with some tobacco in it be allowed to push you around?"

4. Carry a breath spray. A few squirts on the tongue is a refreshing reminder of just how much better your mouth tastes. It's an excellent non-calorie substitute for mint candy.

5. Imagine for a moment what just one drag does to you cilia and your lungs. You understand now why smoking inhibits and ultimately destroys the cilia so they are unable to get rid of the mucus, and you are thus forced to hack it up in spasms of coughing. Every day of non-smoking allows the cilia to improve their functioning and reduces your coughing.

6. Keep in mind that 10,000,000 people have quit in the last 5 years. So can you.

7. From time to time, sit down and write out all the reasons for your quitting. Reminding yourself how many there are and how important they are, will strengthen your *decision*.

7
DON'T SIT BACK AND RELAPSE
(one little cigarette can't hurt)

"We learn from history that we learn nothing from history."

Hegel

Recidivism (ree-syd-ah-vism): what happens to nearly 4 out of 5 smokers who quit.

Unpreparedness: character flaw common to most fallen ex-smokers.

When you quit smoking, it is important to comprehend fully that, like the ex-alcoholic who must never succumb to another drink, you should never even play at smoking another cigarette. To be sure, you may happen across a reformed smoker who can light up from time to time and get away with it. But he is a rare individual indeed and probably was a very light smoker to begin with. For each of these "Now I do, now I don't" ambidextrous cigarette virtuosos, there are a dozen

s of failed ex-smokers who capitulated after as
ly as ten smoke-free years.

The purpose of this chapter is to prepare you for certain unanticipated situations that can quite suddenly vitiate your resolve and leave you defenseless and, once again, puffing away like the idiot you used to be.

SECOND AND THIRD MONTH AFTER QUIT DAY

During these crucial months, when the worst is definitely behind, you may experience moments of intense desire for a cigarette which come upon you most unexpectedly. These are disturbing and dangerous occasions because they are replays, infrequent to be sure, of the insatiable hunger you conquered during those first difficult weeks. The intensity of the desire may be a surprise. Don't let it induce a defeatist attitude which becomes a rationale for giving up your new freedom. It is important to be aware that this may happen, and it is important to understand that the intensity and frequency will steadily decrease with time.

During the early weeks, you may enjoy considerable morale-building praise from family, friends and fellow workers. But after several weeks of cigarette-free living, most of this verbal support ceases. Your claque is convinced the battle has been won even though you may still be struggling through one day at a time. After all, they can't keep applauding you week after week for what appears to them to be the single act of stopping on a certain day. They don't cheer Yastrzemski for last week's home run.

As the neophyte ex-smoker moves into the second and third months, he may resent this support slippage. If this should happen to you, it is a sure sign that you haven't quite slammed the door on a possible desertion back to the doom fumes. Be ready for it and kick the door shut hard.

"Always do right. This will gratify some people and astonish the rest."

Mark Twain

B.C. by permission of Johnny Hart and Field Enterprises, Inc.

4 MONTHS TO 4 YEARS AFTER QUIT DAY

Interviews with hundreds of unsuccessful quitters reveal interesting patterns. In general, there appear to be two distinctly different occasions which may trigger the ex-smoker's fall from tar-free grace. Most common is the misplaced confidence of the fume-free convert that he can handle one or two cigarettes without getting hooked again. Sadly, he almost always does get hooked again. He smokes a few at a party Saturday night, just for the hell of it. He is a little surprised at how good they taste. Since he hadn't smoked a single cigarette for a long time, he assumed they would now taste like a smouldering dog collar. Sunday, he borrows a couple of butts from a neighbor. Nothing serious, you understand. Monday, he bums cigarettes from fellow workers, just a few. The moment of truth arrives around Wednesday or Thursday. He finds himself standing at the cigarette counter and hears a voice that can't possibly be his ordering a package of cigarettes. And how many times have we heard the rationale "Well, I went cold turkey once. I can always do it again." So can any accomplished masochist.

> "We should be careful to get out of an experience only the wisdom that is in it — and stop there; lest we be like the cat that sits down on the hot stove-lid. She will never sit down on the hot stove-lid again — and that is well; but also she will never sit down on a cold one anymore."
>
> *Mark Twain*

Among other failed ex-smokers, we find reasons that are at least more meaningful than simply lighting up at a party "for the hell of it." These more understandable reasons usually revolve around some kind of crisis, at work or in the family; getting fired or divorced, accidents, ill health, etc. An ex-smoker coming under heavy personal pressure can easily reach for the little white pacifier. The pattern is then similar to our party-puffer, and in a few days he's putting coins in a cigarette vending machine and cursing himself.

Everything in this chapter is intended to forewarn the successful quitter, to alert him to the most common situations which can insidiously rekindle the flame and the shame months and even years after a smoker has won the battle.

PART III

MOST EVERYTHING YOU NEVER WANTED TO KNOW ABOUT CIGARETTES AND DIDN'T KNOW WHO TO ASK

"If you think that one individual can't make a difference in the world, consider what one cigar can do in a nine-room house."
Bill Vaughan, Nana

Maya civilization at its height A.D. 470-620

1

PUFF!
THE MAGIC DRAG ON
A BRIEF HISTORY OF THE CIGARETTE

"A cigarette is the perfect type of a perfect pleasure. It is exquisite, and it leaves one unsatisfied. What more can one want?"
Oscar Wilde

History has it that in 500 B.C. the Greek historian, Herodotus, had a penchant for sprinkling hemp (marijuana) seeds over hot stones and sniffing the smoke. This is not only the first recorded high Greek but immediately brings to mind the current definition of "stoned." Herodotus was a head in more ways than one.

We know that sniffing and inhaling various kinds of smoke goes back for thousands of years, although tobacco didn't arrive in Europe until the middle of the

Drinking and Smoking Bout in Amsterdam at the Beginning of the Seventeenth Century

Engraving on copper. From "Bacchus Wonderwerken" Amsterdam, 1628
From the collection of S. Feinhals, Cologne.

16th century. It was, in fact, Christopher Columbus and his crew who first reported seeing Indians "drinking smoke" through a y-shaped pipe called a taboca.

Some time around 1550, a Frenchman, André de Thevet, brought back some tobacco seeds from South America and planted them in his garden. Tobacco was indigenous to the Americas, and it is believed this was its initial introduction to Europe. The subject is controversial, for at about the same time a French envoy to Portugal was actively distributing the seeds to the aristocracy and encouraging the use of tobacco for medicinal purposes. Although history has nearly forgotten the gentleman, his name lives on — Jean Nicot.

In the late sixteenth century, English explorers had observed Nicaraguan Indian women smoking rolled tobacco leaves. They related this habit to the sexual ardor and passion they experienced with these women and proceeded at once to ship tobacco back home. By 1614, London had 7,000 tobacco shops plus, no doubt, numerous puzzled and frustrated wishful thinkers.

Europeans began using tobacco in much the same way as the Indians in North, South and Central America had been doing for centuries — chewing it, sniffing it and smoking it in pipes.

Tobacco was not universally welcomed. In 1604, King James I of England published his "Counter Blaste to Tobacco" about "this stinking smoke." The King wrote: "A custome lothsome to the eye, hatefull to the nose, harmefull to the braine, dangerous to the lungs..." With today's knowledge, many would agree that the King was indeed a prophet. So, perhaps, was this anonymous author:

Popularity of Cigar-smoking in London, 1827

English copper plate. From the collection of J. Feinhals, Cologne

"Tobacco is an evil weed.
It was the devil sowed the seed;
It stains your fingers, burns your clothes
And makes a chimney of your nose."

With a different point of view and lacking today's facts, Charles Lamb wrote with unintentional irony —

"For thy sake, Tobacco, I
Would do anything but die."

Early in the nineteenth century, cigars began to be produced in New Orleans for home consumption, and around 1810 the Cuban cigar made its debut with considerable success. This began the century of the cigar. Again, not everyone thought this was progress. The famous newspaper publisher, Horace Greeley, described the cigar as "a fire at one end and a fool at the other."

Notwithstanding the many efforts over the centuries to halt the spread of tobacco, its popularity thrived. A key reason for its expansion was its enormous value to various governments who profited from the monopolies and taxes on tobacco. A striking example of its value to the state can be found in the order issued in 1851 by Cardinal Giacomo Antonelli, Secretary to the Papal States, to the effect that no one was to put any obstacle in the way of smoking. Anyone distributing anti-smoking literature was to be imprisoned. The use of tobacco in all forms was becoming more socially acceptable.

Chewing tobacco, for example, became very popular in the United States. The spittoon was a fairly common household accessory, and a man with an accurate aim was more cheerfully tolerated. Not until 1921 did cigarettes achieve more popularity than chewing tobacco, pipe tobacco and cigars.

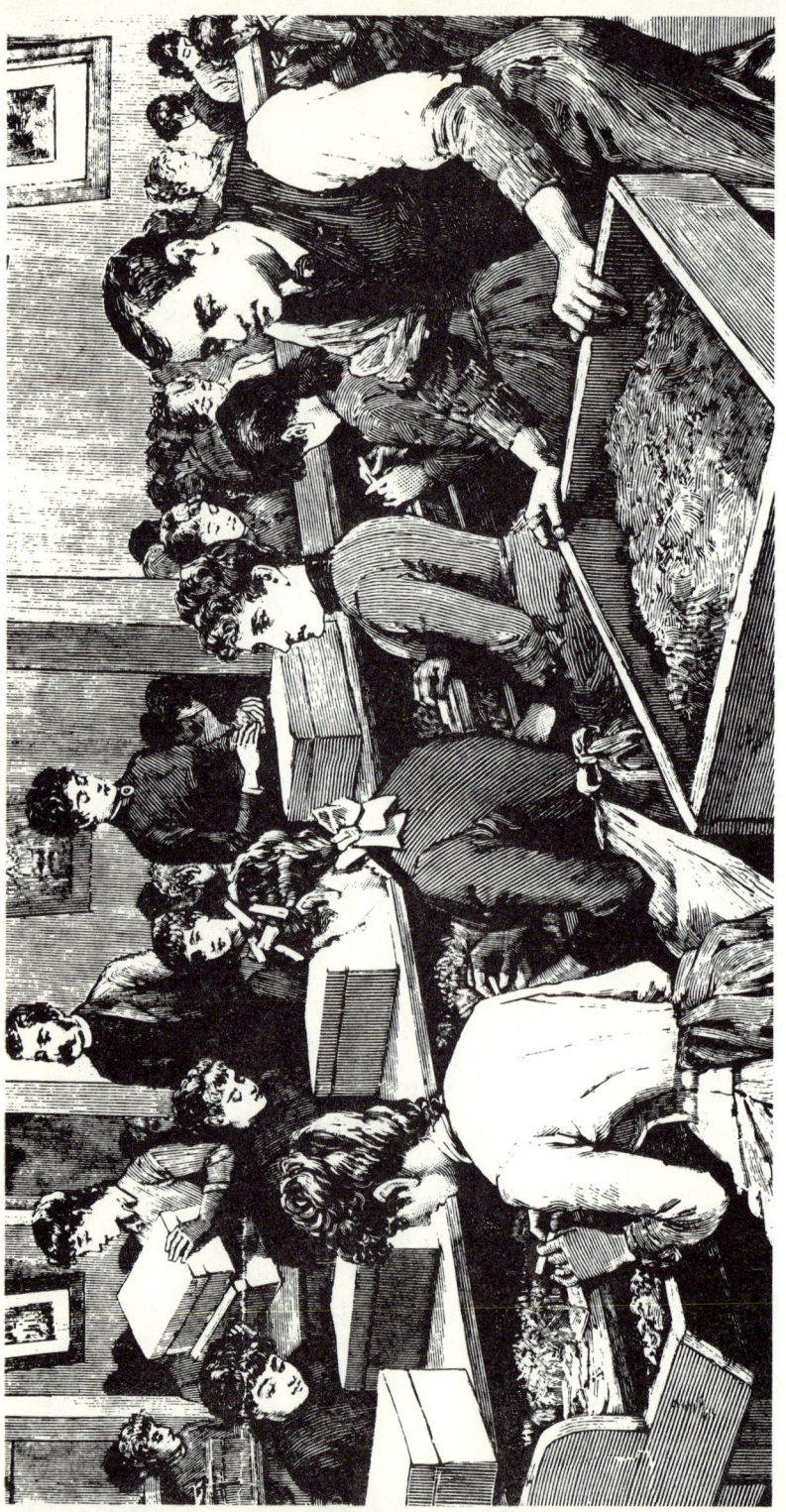

Wood cut of factory women hand rolling cigarettes — 1875
The Bettmann Archive

Exactly when and where the cigarette came into being is uncertain. The term "cigar-ette" would certainly seem to have originated with the French to describe a small cigar. Some daring ladies did smoke small cigars in the 1800's, with George Sand perhaps the most notorious. There is some question as to when "cigarette" referred exclusively to shredded tobacco rolled in paper. Centuries before, native Americans were known to have smoked crushed tobacco stuffed in reeds, quite probably the first crude cigarette.

Peasants in 19th century Europe used to chop up the tobacco from discarded cigar butts and wrap this mixture in scrap paper. These aromatic leftovers were called cigarillos. Rolling your own cost less than buying cigars and, using a more legitimate source of tobacco, the custom caught on. In Great Britain in 1856, an Englishman opened the first cigarette factory, and this new form of smoking, which would ultimately dominate the tobacco industry, was officially in business.

In the long history of smoking, the cigarette as we know it today, is a relative newcomer. It was in Durham, North Carolina, less than a hundred years ago that an event took place which was to revolutionize the production and ultimately the distribution and promotion of cigarettes. In 1884, Washington Duke, having leased a new cigarette machine invented by James Bonsack of Virginia, began producing the incredible total of 120,000 cigarettes a day. This was about fifty times more than the women and young girls in the various New York shops could produce on hand machines.

The Duke Company plowed its profits into promotion, and soon their brands were selling across the country.

These were the good old days before the Sherman Anti-Trust Act, and by 1890 Duke had combined with or swallowed up his four largest competitors and formed the American Tobacco Company. They manufactured between 75% and 90% of all tobacco products consumed in the United States.

In 1911, a Supreme Court decision broke up this near monopoly into four separate and competing companies: American, Liggett & Myers, Lorillard, and Reynolds. If one overlooks the diseases and deaths caused by tobacco, it has been mostly fun and profits ever since.

Before World War I, smokers preferred the more exotic Near Eastern blends, and leading brand names reflected this — *Fatima, Omar, Zubelda, Egyptian Straights*. In 1913, Reynolds introduced a new American blend with the brand name *Camel*. Early tests were so successful that Reynolds concentrated most of his advertising and promotion dollars behind this one brand. By 1918, R.J. Reynolds had 40% of the cigarette market. Three brands dominated the field: Reynolds' "I'd Walk a Mile for a Camel;" American Tobacco's "Lucky Strike, It's Toasted;" Liggett & Myers' "Chesterfields — They Satisfy."

When his father died in 1925, George Washington Hill took over the American Tobacco Company. He would become the most notorious and controversial figure in the cigarette industry. For example, it is reported that he once wrote of the "sheep dip" in his competitors' brands. It was Hill who coined the slogan "Reach for a Lucky instead of a sweet" and started many an innocent and, perhaps, plump damsel on the cigarette habit. Naturally, the candy manufacturers were furious, and after years of battling them, Hill cut the phrase to "Reach for a Lucky instead." In the end, the F.T.C. stepped in and forbade any slogan that implied cigarettes were a reducing device. But by 1931, Lucky Strike was No. 1 and would continue to be either first or second vs. Camel until 1950. Chesterfield, Old Gold and Philip Morris completed the big five.

In the July, 1957 issue of *Reader's Digest*, there was a strong article on the mounting medical evidence against smoking. The advertising agency for *Reader's Digest* was a Madison Avenue shop in New York City. Another client was the American Tobacco Company. On July 17, 1957, about three weeks after the article came out, the agency resigned the magazine account. This is the same agency which produced a special campaign for Lucky Strike in response to growing objections to copy lines that appealed to youth. Picture, if you will, a two-page spread; on the left, a racing car driver is surrounded by young men; on the right, the same driver finds himself in a group of adoring young females. The headline (which was not supposed to appeal to youth) proclaims "Lucky Strike separates the men from the boys . . . but not from the girls."

In spite of medical scares and modest restrictions by the government, the sale of cigarettes reached an all-time high of 607 billion in 1975. The tobacco industry continues to enjoy booming profits, and it must warm and steady their hearts if not their halos to see our children, at an ever younger age, getting hooked on the most serious medical problem in America, the pernicious cigarette.

Smoke as a Cure for Illness

From *Americae Partes*

This picture shows the method employed by the American aborigines in treating the sick, as described in the following words:

"They prepare a sort of long wooden couch on which the sufferers are laid, some on their backs, some on their bellies, according to the nature of their complaints; they then make an incision in the skin of the face with a sharpened oyster shell, suck out the blood, and eject it, time after time, into an earthen vessel. Pregnant women or those who are suckling their infants will assemble to drink this blood, especially if it be that of a vigorous young man, in order that their milk may be of a better quality, and their children grow stronger and more valiant in consequence.

Other patients will lie on their bellies and inhale the smoke from tobacco sprinkled on live coals; this taken in through the mouth and nostrils, and so diffused throughout the entire body, produces vomiting, and removes the cause of suffering.

They have also a plant the Spanish call *Tabak*; when the leaves have been thoroughly dried, they pack the stuff into the broad end of a tube, light it, put the narrow end to their mouths, and draw in the smoke so vigorously that it comes out again through the lips and nostrils, thus producing an abundance of moisture. These clouds of smoke are a specific against venereal disease, so that nature would seem to have provided them with her own remedy, close at hand."

2
MALICE IN WONDERLAND

"I don't like money, actually, but it quiets my nerves."
Joe Louis

You are the president of a large advertising agency. A new client appears on your doorstep and announces that he wants you to take over his $20,000,000 account. He informs you that his product is in a very competitive field and has a few minor problems:
1. First off, the product is toxic.
2. Thousands of research studies prove beyond doubt that its use causes the premature death of more than 300,000 men and women in the United States every year.
3. The product is addictive.
4. Although the product is ingested through the mouth, it has absolutely no nutritive value.
5. People who don't use this product, and they are in the majority, find it repulsive and disgusting.
6. The cost of the product is skyrocketing. For the average user, it may easily reach $300 to $400 a year.

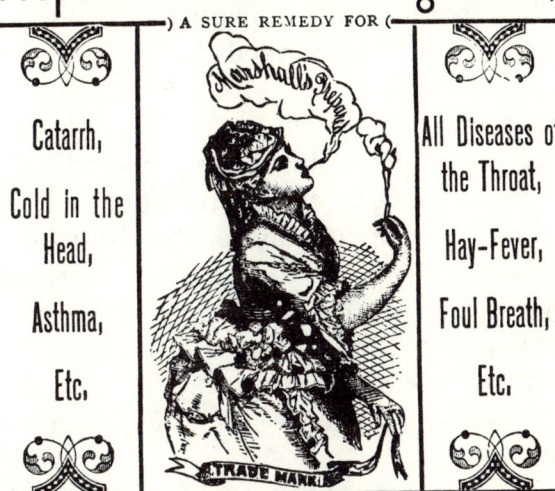

1880 ad describing the curative powers of "Marshall's Celebrated Prepared Cubebs and Cigarettes"

The Bettmann Archive

7. Further costs to the user involve damage to his clothes, his furnishings and, of course, his health.
8. It is estimated that 25% of all damaging fires in the United States are caused by this product. In 1965, a total of 163,900 fires were specifically traced to its use.
9. This product is so damaging to health that the government has banned it from advertising on radio or television.

As your new client continues to list these "minor problems," your enthusiasm has wavered but is still held firmly in place by the magic figure, $20,000,000. He has one more slight drawback to describe:

10. It is now the law of the land that, on the package itself and in all printed ads, there must be a prominent warning that this product "is dangerous to your health."

Now, if you didn't know better, you would have to conclude that:

a. No one could possibly invent a product with such a devastating variety of negatives.

b. If such a troublesome and dangerous product were put on the market, who in his right mind would buy it?

As a matter of fact, in 1900 almost no women and very few men smoked cigarettes. Per capita consumption was 50 cigarettes a year. By 1970, per capita consumption had increased by 80 times and was running at about 4,000 cigarettes a year. This incredible growth is a stunning tribute to the advertising industry, without which it could never have happened.

For here indeed was the ultimate marketing challenge and the black knights of Madison Avenue saw to

1882 English cartoon attacking the "serpent" cigarette
The Bettmann Archive

it that all those "minor problems" were conquered and disappeared, so to speak, in a puff of smoke. When women lagged far behind men in the Russian Roulette of the cigarette world, the ad men came up with the headline, "Blow a little my way," and then a bit later, "Reach for a Lucky instead of a sweet." Women began to close the gap and soon 1 out of every 3 was lighting up with male-like enthusiasm. Many were destined to die prematurely with male-like lack of enthusiasm.

During the 40's and 50's as more and more anti-cigarette articles began to appear in such widely read magazines as the *Reader's Digest* (which still refuses tobacco advertising), the cigarette companies struck back with such questionable slogans that it is hard to believe the government regulatory agencies allowed such misrepresentation:

Old Gold — "Not a cough in a carload,"

Camel — "Not a single case of throat irritation due to smoking Camels,"

Philip Morris — "The throat-tested cigarette," and

Camel — "For digestion's sake, smoke Camels . . . stimulates the flow of digestive juices . . . increases alkalinity."

In March, 1937 the following news item appeared in *The Cleveland Plain Dealer*. Reporters were interviewing the famous opera star, Giovanni Martinelli, when he asked them to extinguish their cigarettes.

"But didn't you endorse a cigarette once?" asked a reporter. "Si, si," admitted the smiling tenor. "But remember what I said: 'These cigarettes never make my throat sore.' And that is true. They never do."

"Because," a reporter suggested, "you never smoke them?"

Turn of the century ad for "High Grade Cigarettes" out of Rochester, New York

The Bettmann Archive

"Si, si," laughed Martinelli, "I never smoke them. I never smoked anything in my life."

"Either these apostles do know that what they promise has only delusional value, yet they want to retain their incomes, or else they live in delusional worlds, and a sane mankind should take care of them."

Alfred Korzybski

In the November 15, 1976 issue of *Advertising Age*, one of the deans of advertising, Walter Weir, tells a fascinating story about George Washington Hill and his No. 1 American Tobacco brand, Lucky Strike. It was 1941 and Mr. Hill had discovered that Chesterfields and Camels were the most popular brands among female smokers although Lucky Strike was still in first place among men. Mr. Weir was given the unenviable assignment of producing an advertising campaign directed to women to correct this sales situation. To keep the challenge prominently in view, Mr. Weir lined up on top of his desk a package of each of the twelve leading cigarette brands.

Quoting Mr. Weir: "Sipping coffee one morning, I saw the packages as I had not seen them before. Three stood out — the Lucky Strike package, which was a dark green, and the Camel and Chesterfield pakages, one of which was white and the other almost white." This inspired him to recommend that Lucky Strike be packaged in white and to feature the headline, "Luckies for the Ladies."

It was about a year later, after Pearl Harbor and our entry into the war, that George Washington Hill finally saw and liked the suggested white package. He requested that the green ink on the present package be chemically analyzed. This revealed that the ink contained an infinitesimal amount of copper. Mr. Hill had recently read a news story relating that old wooden ships were replacing metal ships lost to German submarines. He recalled that wooden ship bottoms were painted with copper to keep out worms, and thus was born one of Mr. Hill's most famous slogans: "Lucky Strike Green has gone to war." Whether it was the white package or the slogan or both, nobody to this day is certain, but within a year the sales of Lucky Strike had risen 29%, primarily because of women smokers.

The white package idea for Luckies at first never got to the client — but when it did, Mr. Hill bought it and added his usual wild touch.

In 1940, there were just 5 big brands — Lucky Strike, Camel, Chesterfield, Old Gold and Philip Morris. They had 95% of the market. By 1969, there were fifteen brands which accounted for about the same percentage of business. Such new names as Kent, Marlboro, Winston and L&M were now leading the pack, and they offered one important change — all came equipped with filters.

In 1953, a very strong article about smoking and lung cancer appeared in *The Journal of the American Medical Association* and helped launch the 50's as the decade of the filter. The filter was for all intents and purposes an invention of the ad industry. With the exception of the original Kent filter, which was later altered to allow more smoke through, the leading brands with filters delivered only slightly less tar and nicotine. Nevertheless, in skilled advertising hands, these inefficient filters were something new with which to dazzle and daze the public.

"The successful advertiser is the master of a new art: the art of making things true by saying they are so."

Daniel Boorstin

The manufacturers were happy because they had a new, though specious, answer to the health scare. What is more, the filter cost less than the tobacco it replaced in the cigarette. The filter also came to the aid of the smoker who now had a new rationalization for what he was reluctantly beginning to realize was a very dangerous habit.

As health claims for the new filters became more strident and confusing, the smoker had little idea which particular brand might actually be safer. Consequently, he chose the filter brand which satisfied him most (frequently the strongest) and believed or pretended that he was better off. The manufacturers continued to loosen up the filters or to add stronger tobacco until finally the F.T.C. announced that it had failed in its statutory duty to "prevent deceptive acts and practices" in filter cigarette advertising.

A "teaser" campaign for Camel Cigarettes around the time of World War I. The top ad might run in the newspaper on Monday, Tuesday and Wednesday, the middle ad on Thursday and the bottom ad on Friday. The Bettmann Archive

The F.T.C. proceeded to obtain voluntary agreements from all the manufacturers to omit health references or tar and nicotine levels from their advertising. This was a boost to the non-filtered brands, and their advertising headlines began to disparage the filter cigarettes:

"Remember how good cigarettes used to taste?"
"No flat filtered-out flavor."
"Smoking more now but enjoying it less?"

Nevertheless, by 1960 filter cigarettes were outselling non-filters, and by 1975 they constituted about 80% of the market. But during those 15 years, all kinds of controversies developed causing the manufacturers and their ad agencies to zig and zag in various directions. There was, for example, the Surgeon General's report in 1964 (an analysis of more than 4,000 reports), the various congressional hearings, the TV anti-cigarette (equal time) commercials, the ban on cigarette advertising for TV and radio, the warning on the package and in ads, the continuing flow of more and more damaging scientific studies.

The tobacco interests were up to the challenge. Advertising budgets dipped temporarily but were soon back moving towards the $300 million level with magazines and newspapers enjoying the former broadcast dollars. While millions of adults continued to bite the bullet and quit, teenage smoking was on the increase, and at an even younger age, with girls leading the way.

There were, however, some positive signs. Moves were under way in Congress to legislate an outright ban on cigarettes with tar levels above 21 mg. Congressmen were studying the innovative New York City cigarette tax which was deliberately increased on brands with high tar and nicotine levels. Non-smokers' rights were finally gaining recognition with State and Federal regulations banning smoking in public places and specified areas in public carriers.

On November 13, 1975, Congressman Drinan of Massachusetts introduced the Smoker and Non-Smoker Health Protection Act (H.R. 10748) to safeguard the rights of non-smokers and to strengthen the provisions of the Cigarette Labeling and Advertising Act of 1965. Congressman Drinan wrote as follows: "Recently, medical research has begun to document the effects of smoking upon the 150 million Americans who don't smoke. Most non-smokers who find themselves breathing the smoke emitted by others in elevators, offices, conference rooms, restaurants, and other public places suffer in silence though it may cause their eyes to water, their noses to itch, and their heads to ache.

"I have heard from hundreds of individuals who have had to quit their jobs or curtail their social activities because of adverse reactions to smoke-contaminated air. More than 30 states, including Massachusetts, have recognized the seriousness of this problem by enacting legislation to restrict smoking in public places.

"H.R. 10748 would require all federal agencies to adopt regulations to separate smokers from non-smokers to the extent possible in offices, lounges, and cafeterias and to prohibit smoking altogether in other indoor areas open to the public. Federal office buildings, courtrooms, post offices, military bases, and Congress itself would be among the thousands of facilities covered by the bill. Similar provisions would apply to airports, bus terminals, train stations, and port facilities engaged in interstate commerce.

"The formulation of legislation in this field involves a delicate balance between the right of an individual to smoke and the right of his or her neighbor to breathe air which is relatively uncontaminated by tar, carbon monoxide, formaldehyde, and other substances contained in tobacco smoke. H.R. 10748 is designed to protect the majority of Americans who don't smoke without preventing smokers from lighting up in private, out-of-doors, and in designated smoking areas."

There was a grudging realization by tobacco manufacturers that the rules of the game were changing in spite of their huge lobbying efforts and the clout of the tobacco-growing states. New low tar brands began to proliferate, and the race was on for this growing share of the market. 9 mg. tar Merit was successfully launched with one of the largest ad budgets in history, estimated at $40 million. Kent Golden Lights jumped in with one less mg. tar at 8. At the lowest level, American Tobacco's Carlton at 4 mg. had been moving well with a 27% sales increase in 1973 which continued in 1974 and 1975. R. J. Reynolds saw the possibilities and introduced Now at only 2 mg. Carlton could no longer proclaim in ads that it was lowest in tar so they adjusted their tar levels down to 2 mg. and headlined "Nobody's lower than Carlton." Shortly thereafter, both Carlton and Now reduced to 1 mg. tar.

However, handsome men and women still looked you straight in the eye and declared they smoked Winstons for taste. The tattooed cowboy in Marlboro Country still sat on his horse and lit up as the sun went down.

Tareyton, with its charcoal filter which delivered a generous 17 mg. tar, declared: "Others remove. Tareyton improves." And America's teenagers and adults continued to exist in an environment which sanctioned cigarette smoking as not only legal but socially acceptable and just possibly the "in" thing to do. 607 billion cigarettes were sold to Americans in 1975.

Mr. Emerson Foote, the former president of the largest advertising firm in this country, put it this way: "Basically, the promotion of cigarette smoking is a clear application of the principle of the primacy of profits over people. In one way or another, the disastrous effects of cigarette advertising on the health of our people, present and future, must be done away with."

The cynicism of the advertising fraternity is, perhaps, best reflected in a front-page article in *Advertising Age* April 19, 1976. In a bicentennial piece on advertising in colonial times, A. Stanley Kramer stated: "Nor did these early ads consciously play on the hidden wellsprings of human behavior. Almost naively, advertisers said what they meant, and meant what they said."

Although all cigarette tobacco is heat treated or "toasted" in one way or another, it was the American Tobacco Company who dramatically announced that Lucky Strike was "toasted." 1929

"Light a Lucky and you'll never miss sweets that make you fat"

Constance Talmadge

Constance Talmadge,
Charming Motion
Picture Star

INSTEAD of eating between meals...instead of fattening sweets...beautiful women keep youthful slenderness these days by smoking Luckies. The smartest and loveliest women of the modern stage take this means of keeping slender...when others nibble fattening sweets, they light a Lucky!

Lucky Strike is a delightful blend of the world's finest tobaccos. These tobaccos are toasted—a costly extra process which develops and improves the flavor. That's why Luckies are a delightful alternative for fattening sweets. That's why there's real health in Lucky Strike. That's why folks say: "It's good to smoke Luckies."

For years this has been no secret to those men who keep fit and trim. They know that Luckies steady their nerves and do not harm their physical condition. They know that Lucky Strike is the favorite cigarette of many prominent athletes, who must keep in good shape. They respect the opinions of 20,679 physicians who maintain that Luckies are less irritating to the throat than other cigarettes.

A reasonable proportion of sugar in the diet is recommended, but the authorities are overwhelming that too many fattening sweets are harmful and that too many such are eaten by the American people. So, for moderation's sake we say:—

"REACH FOR A LUCKY
INSTEAD OF A SWEET."

Constance Talmadge,
Charming Motion
Picture Star

"It's toasted"
No Throat Irritation-No Cough.

Reach for a Lucky instead of a sweet.

In 1929, Lucky Strike also introduced the phrase "Reach for a Lucky instead of a sweet" which, not surprisingly, infuriated the candy manufacturers.   The Bettmann Archive

125

In 1930, Lucky Strike tried to placate the candy interests by shortening their slogan to "Reach for a Lucky instead —." At the same time, they introduced the fat man and fat woman "Shadows of the Future."

In 1931, Lucky Strike suggested you "Consider your Adam's Apple" and continued to recommend you "Reach for a Lucky instead."

In another 1931 campaign, the Lucky Strike advertising copy once again concentrated on the superior quality when "It's Toasted."

In 1937, this ad in McCall's Magazine reflected the social respectability of the lowly cigarette as well as the exploitability of high society.

3
$MOKE GETS IN THEIR AYES

"Many politicians give the impression that their every action is designed to comfort the comfortable and oppress the oppressed."
Anonymous

The United States government does not have an enviable record in the cigarette controversy. Although Congress may yet redeem itself, over the years various government agencies, and most particularly the Executive Office, have been most reluctant to disturb the tobacco interests.

In October, 1974 President Ford illustrated typical presidential inaction caused by sensitivity to the tobacco lobby. In spite of the overwhelming evidence against tar and nicotine, he stated in a letter: "It should be pointed out that there is considerable dispute as to whether there exists adequate scientific evidence on which to base safe levels of tar and nicotine under responsible regulatory action." The tobacco industry couldn't have said it better.

The Carter administration appears to be equally confused and compromised. The following excerpts from the editorial page of *The New York Times*, Nov. 20, 1977, demonstrate the grotesque irresponsibility still emanating from the Executive Office. The *Times* reported that when Dr. Julius B. Richmond, the Surgeon General, addressed a conference sponsored by the American Cancer Society, he stressed the death and disability that result from cigarette smoking — and the likelihood that smoking ailments will cost the nation $20 billion this year. . . .The burden of the message was clear: nothing would improve the health of the American people more than the elimination of cigarette smoking.

But when Dr. Peter G. Bourne, President Carter's Special Assistant for Health Issues, handed in a paper to a Cancer Society committee later the same day, it showed him on a remarkably different track; President Carter is "very concerned" about tobacco hazards, Dr. Bourne said, but he also believes "the American people have been adequately warned." While the federal government has a reponsibility to minimize the hazards, it must also be "responsive to our 600,000 farm families who derive their income from tobacco." Federally funded programs to help people quit smoking may be "too costly." Nor should we always assume the worst about tobacco — some of its components may be "beneficial."

Senator Maurine Neuberger in her excellent book "Smoke Screen: Tobacco and the Public Welfare" (1963, Prentice-Hall) reveals just how inactive Congress was in the tobacco and health area. "The Library of Congress succeeded in unearthing for me some thirty legis-

Reprinted by permissions of Ben Sargent and the Austin American-Statesman.

lative proposals designed to treat various aspects of the smoking problem which have been, at one time or another, laid before Congress. . . .

"My husband, the late Senator Richard Neuberger, was the author of two of these bills. Dick considered it a scandalous anomaly that tobacco was *supported* as one of America's 'six basic crops' at the very time that the public health arm of the federal government was bearing witness to its harm.

"No bill relating to the smoking problem has ever been accorded even a perfunctory hearing. Each was permanently and unceremoniously interred in committee."

Senator Neuberger also describes "a particularly odious column" which her husband unearthed in the magazine, *"Tobacco, The International Weekly of Industry and Science":*

"Here's something new the cigarette industry must face: New York City's Bureau of Public Health Education has completed a program to deter school children and teenagers from smoking. . . . The disturbing factor about the New York City school anti-smoking educational drive is that other cities might follow. It might deter all children from ever becoming smokers."

That completely cynical statement from the tobacco industry was made in the early 60's. They had nothing to worry about. Youngsters, starting as early as 11 and 12, continue to take up cigarette smoking in increasing numbers. The largest increase is among young females, which prompted someone to describe them as "pretty young girls in their early nicotines."

Senator Neuberger does single out one government employee who made a lonely and courageous decision.

In October 1962, Air Force Surgeon General, Major General Oliver Niess, ordered the termination of free cigarettes in Air Force hospitals and clinics and in-flight lunches. As the Senator points out: "To the tobacco industry, the chilling message of Surgeon General Niess' action was that a responsible official, acting upon sound medical testimony, was beyond the reach of all the economic power and political pressure that the industry could muster."

However, most government agencies and the people running them have tended to ignore the increasing scientific proof about cigarette smoking and health. Here are some examples that reflect this attitude.

The Federal Food and Drug Administration has wide responsibilities as its title suggests. Although it was responsible for tobacco at one time, it appears the tobacco states traded some votes years ago, and it was removed. How exciting to know that at a later date chewing gum was added.

Some years ago, Congressman Abbitt inserted a newspaper article in the Congressional Record. The headline read: "U. S. Aide fights cigarette scares." Who was this aide who urged citizens to "sit back, relax and smoke a cigarette?" Why, he was Chief of the Tobacco Division of the Agriculture Department's Marketing Services. The article finished by saying: "The Agricultural Department Official calls the tobacco health scare a big smokescreen."

We still have one government agency looking after the interests of the tobacco grower and another agency trying to discourage the use of tobacco. Congressman Drinan (Mass., Democrat) effectively exposed this hypocrisy in a speech to the House of Representatives on November 13, 1975:

"The federal government continues to pay large subsidies to tobacco growers even as it proclaims that smoking is dangerous to health. More than $60 million was spent last year to help the tobacco industry produce more of its unhealthy product. Farmers are encouraged to grow as much tobacco as possible since the Government guarantees a federal price support. While medical evidence demonstrating the danger of smoking to health has mounted during the past 10 years, tobacco subsidies have risen 34%.

"The Department of Agriculture helps to promote the export of cigarettes on behalf of the tobacco industry. Incredibly, the Department ships thousands of tons of tobacco to foreign nations under the so-called 'Food for Peace' program which was designed to help starving people overseas to regain their good health, not to bring them additional sickness through a certified health hazard. It is difficult to take a government seriously when it talks so blatantly out of both sides of its mouth."

That excerpt is from an important speech by Congressman Drinan when he introduced his bill "The Smoker and Non-Smoker Health Protection Act of 1975." Among other things, this bill would:

a) greatly strengthen the cigarette package warning;
b) require tar and nicotine content on every package;
c) require all cigarette advertising to carry a) and b) above;
d) allow states to control cigarette advertising;
e) give non-smokers vastly increased protection; and

f) increase the federal excise tax on cigarettes by a penny a pack with the proceeds used to expand medical research by the National Heart and Living Institute into smoking-related diseases.

Columnist Ellen Goodman in *The Boston Globe* skillfully exposed the absurdity of the government's position in relation to the controversy concerning the ban on saccharin.

"I don't seem to be able to get all warm and wiggly about the federal government's concern over my health. After years of hearing about red dye, sodium nitrite, flame-resistant children's pajamas, etc., the banning business looks more like a lottery than like the result of a rational program of research. By now our confidence is so undermined that most Americans greet the saccharin news with a philosophical 'Well, what doesn't give you cancer?'

"Amidst all the conflict and confusion, the question that keeps recycling in my mind is this: How does one branch of government ban a product proven to cause bladder cancer in a few cases, while another branch of government subsidizes a product that causes lung cancer?

"While saccharin has caused cancer in rats in Canada, tobacco is inexorably linked to cancer, emphysema, and heart disease in people in the United States. How is it that one is regulated and not the other?

"Well, it turns out that the answer is as flaky as it is simple. The FDA doesn't regulate tobacco because you don't eat it, smear it over your body, or take it to cure an ailment.

Copyright 1977 by Herblock in The Washington Post.

"The Food, Drug and Cosmetics Act covers only, you guessed it, food, drugs and cosmetics. If manufacturers put tobacco in a moisturizing cream, a candy bar or a pill, the FDA could take it off the market. But while you do put cigarettes in your mouth, you don't normally eat them. You only swallow the smoke, which is not a food, and therefore by this same inane logic, not a matter of agency concern.

"I suppose that if you snorted saccharin it would still be on the market.

"The Delaney Amendment says that any food or drug which is found to cause cancer (no matter how rarely) in humans or animals must be banned. So the FDA had no choice in the matter of saccharin. But the only thing regulating cigarettes is the so-called 'free enterprise' system.

"Just how 'free' this enterprise is, is another question.

"The government allots $80 million a year in subsidies to those who grow tobacco. We even pay to send some of it abroad in what is called our Food For Peace program. (Of course, tobacco isn't a food, you remember, but. . . .)

"Curiouser and curiouser, while one part of the government is spending this $80 million to subsidize tobacco, another part is spending $2 million a year on a campaign to prevent people from smoking it.

"Moreover, (I warned you this wouldn't be easy), according to the resident gadfly at the Public Citzen's Health Research Institute, Dr. Sidney Wolfe, we are spending between $11 billion and $14 billion a year for the morbidity costs, the direct medical costs and the mortality costs related to smoking."

By permission of Chicago Tribune-New York News Syndicate.

On January 29, 1976, Senator Gary Hart of Colorado and Senator Edward Kennedy of Massachusetts introduced the National Health Research and Development Act of 1976 in order to insure continued advances in the diagnosis, treatment, and prevention of disease. This activity would be funded by a new health tax on cigarettes. The amount of the health tax for any given brand of cigarettes would be determined by the tar and nicotine content of the brand. In the first year, the strongest cigarettes would cost 20 cents more per pack. The average tax on all brands would be 12 cents. By 1980, the health tax would range from 2 cents to 50 cents per pack with an average of 30 cents per pack.

If this proposal or something similar becomes law, successful readers of THE SECOND-BEST SMOKING PLAN are going to enjoy significant savings.

But, of course, the tobacco industry will battle furiously to defeat both of these desperately needed bills.

4
PIT STOP ON TOBACCO ROAD

A chef who was asked for the recipe of his famous corn beef hash replied: "There is no recipe. The stuff simply accumulates."

When the skillful fingers of women and young girls hand-rolled cigarettes one hundred years ago, they were using imported linen paper from France and unadulterated tobacco leaf from here and abroad. (They rolled about 15,000 per week for which they were paid a maximum of $9.) Today, your cigarette tobacco may be homogenized, puffed, washed with acids, and bathed in a wide variety of chemical flavorings. Your filter may be carbonactivated, perforated, channeled, recessed, and occasionally ineffective. But let's start with the tobacco plant itself to find out what's been happening.

To begin with, 5-inch seedlings are hand or machine planted in carefully prepared soil, which is occasionally fumigated beforehand. In about five months the plants are 4 to 8 feet tall and ready for harvesting. Either the individual leaves or the entire plant is hung from a stick or wire in a fairly airtight barn where the curing takes place. This process improves taste, aroma and burning quality. The most popular method is flue-curing which involves heat from exterior fires being distributed by pipes or flues throughout the barn's interior for a period of about 3 days. In the next process, called stripping, the leaves are moistened to prevent cracking and then removed from the stem. The leaves are bundled into "hands" and stored in bales or casks ready for the tobacco auction. The purchaser will then redry the tobacco to a moisture content of 10%. It is now ready for the final aging process and will be repacked and stored away for one or two years.

When the "hands" are fully aged, the stems and veins are removed, and the leaves are cut into strips. Strips of various types of tobacco are then mixed together. Moisture-enhancing substances such as apple juice or glycerine, and flavorings such as mint or menthol, are sometimes added to the blends at this time. Methods have now been developed whereby the waste products such as stems and veins can be ground up and homogenized. It can then be blended with inferior tobaccos into a mash which is rolled out in paper-like sheets ready for shredding and stuffing into someone's favorite brand.

Menthol brands make up 29% of the United States market. The volatility of natural and synthetic menthol creates problems for the manufacturer: i.e., contamination of unmentholated tobacco products during manufacture, shorter shelf life for menthol cigarettes, migration of the menthol flavor from the tobacco to the filter, uneven release of the menthol when the cigarette is burning. The manufacturer can at least be relieved that to date there is no evidence that menthol in any way increases the danger of the smoke.

An incredible variety of flavors has been tested in tobacco to improve or to camouflage various blends. For example, in the book "Tobacco Flavoring Substances and Methods" published by Noyes Data Corp., we find the following in one chapter alone: mint, spicy, woody, camphor, fruity and flowery, cocoa and chocolate. Chemical names such as cyclohexylcylohexanone have been left out of this list due to a shortage of paper and patience.

Great Britain bans the use of any additive other than water, and their cigarettes are made entirely of flue-cured tobacco. Manufacturers in the United States are mixing the tobacco with every conceivable type of chemical, and when one asks for some specifics, they are usually told that these are "aromatic hydrocarbons."

The Department of H.E.W. through its National Cancer Institute has a continuing program to make available to cigarette manufacturers the most promising chemical flavoring system for application to low-tar cigarettes. Dr. Gio B. Gori, Deputy Director of the National Cancer Institute, is in charge of the effort which is pursued under government contract at the world-famous Arthur D. Little, Inc. in Cambridge, Mass. Anne Neilson, Director of this project, explains that their "flavor profile" approach has been operating for more than twenty-five years and has investigated the flavors and odors of everything from high and low calorie colas to diesel fumes.

For nearly three years, Arthur D. Little has been "flavor profiling" hundreds of different chemical combinations in a search for the most effective and most acceptable cigarette flavor. Many of the most successful combinations have been published by H.E.W. in their annual reports, and some may already be in use by cigarette manufacturers. The companies, of course, will not reveal their individual formulas, but certainly the work being done by the chemists and tasters at Arthur D. Little will be very important in making low-tar brands more satisfying and more readily accepted by the average smoker.

The filter-tipped cigarette originated in Central Europe. In 1952, it accounted for only 1.4% of production in the United States, by 1970, 70% of domestic production was filter tipped. Because the filter makes it more difficult to draw air through the cigarette, the tobacco must be more loosely packed. One answer has been the use of puffed tobacco. Although it has never shown up in the retail price, manufacturers have steadily reduced their costs by giving the smoker less tobacco, partly through loose packing and partly because the less expensive filter replaces what would be tobacco.

YEAR	AVERAGE WEIGHT OF TOBACCO PER 1,000 CIGARETTES
1954	2.700 lbs.
1964	2.197 lbs.
1974	1.907 lbs.
1975	1.874 lbs.

U.S. Dept. of Agriculture

While the tobacco content went down, cigarette sales went up:

YEAR	BILLION/UNITS
1971	547.2
1972	561.7
1973	584.7
1974	594.5
1975	603.4 (Est.)

F.T.C.

Since filter cigarettes now dominate the market, it is interesting to note the many imaginative types of filters that have been created. One rather clever and effective innovation is found in the filter on Decade cigarettes (5 mg. tar). Their advertising describes it this way: "Unique 'taste channel' gives first puff impact. The Decade filter is a combination of laser technology, plus our own exclusive research design. Simply, we've created a channel within the filter to give you that first puff impact you've come to expect from only the high 'tar' cigarettes. Which means you get taste from first puff to last."

What all that flashy rhetoric means is that if you cut open the filter you will find a small plastic tube which allows a metered amount of unfiltered smoke to pass directly to the smoker. It works rather well, and the brand's success reflects it.

Another ingeniously designed filter contains one or more circles of perforations located midway in the filter so that the lips would not normally cover them while smoking. When ventilating air is introduced through the filter perforations, the principal effect is that less air passes through the burning end during the puff. This change is responsible for the differing effect on the yields of various smoke components. Most yields go down significantly, although nicotine is reduced somewhat less than others. The decrease in deadly carbon monoxide is larger than might be anticipated. Overall, the perforated filter is an important step towards a less harmful cigarette.

We have traveled a long way from the lady at the rolling table who, using the palm of her hand, could with one motion shape a cigarette ready for gluing. In 1955, American cigarettes delivered on average 43 mg. tar and 2.8 mg. nicotine. These levels dropped to 18 mg. tar and 1.2 mg. nicotine in 1975. From all indications, the furious activity along tobacco road will continue in the direction of less injurious but in reality still *very* lethal cigarettes.

THE PROBLEM

A SHORT ACCOUNT OF A NON-SMOKER'S DILEMMA

MAD MAGAZINE
September 1975

(C) 1975 By
E. C. Publications, Inc.

3

4

5
SMOKE RINGS FROM THE DOOM FUMES

NEWS RELEASES FROM THE TOBACCO FRONT

"And then there was the cigarette addict who announced that he had read so many terrible things about smoking that he decided to give up reading."

Playboy Magazine

August 9, 1974 Reuter News Service
The Celanese Corporation of America has created a new product called Cytrel. Wood pulp is fed into machinery which changes it by a patented process and sends out what looks like inch square pieces of brown

paper. Cytrel contains no nicotine and 1/3 to 1/7 the amount of tar in tobacco and will produce virtually no poisonous gases such as carbon monoxide.

In the company's consumer tests, Cytrel is shredded and moistened and mixed, in proportions ranging from 20% to 40%, with tobacco and then made into cigarettes.

70% of the group tested actually preferred the 20% to 40% Cytrel mix to their regular brand.

Because of some reluctance on the part of American cigarette companies to use non-tobacco substances, this will be tested by British cigarette manufacturers in Great Britain. When Dr. Gio Bata Gori of the National Cancer Institute was asked why the United States appeared to be lagging behind in developing a substitute for tobacco, he said: "In a word, the United States is a major producer of tobacco."

July 1973 Associated Press

Australians have produced a new cigarette filter made from pure wool. Tests at the University of New South Wales show the wool filter is 18% more effective than synthetic filters. Around 20 million pounds of raw wool would be needed a year if Australian cigarette manufacturers switched to the new filter.

January 19, 1976 London Express News Service

The long search for nicotine-free cigarettes which taste exactly like the real thing was claimed yesterday by a group of Israeli scientists in Jerusalem. Their patented product, made from dried lettuce leaves, will be called "Long Life." They report it also has 50% less tar.

Dr. Max Scheib, a member of the research team, said they can produce any type and flavor cigarette — "from the strong cigarettes which the French like to Virginia-type blends for British and American smokers."

January 15, 1976
According to a recent United States Public Health Service report, there are 49 million American smokers and 37 million — or 75% — want to quit.

"All mankind is divided into three classes: Those who are immovable; those who are movable; and those who move."
Benjamin Franklin

All cigarette addicts know the smoking ritual: one on awakening, one with the first cup of coffee, one after breakfast, and so on. The uptight housewife, off cigarettes for 2 weeks, when asked the time by her husband snapped back: "It's two cigarettes after eight."

An organization called ASH, Action on Smoking and Health, was formed by the young lawyer, John Banzhaf, who successfully got equal time for anti-cigarette commercials on television. Any smoker with children during those years knows how devastating those commercials were. ASH continues to be very influential in the battle against smoking, banning cigarette advertisers from TV and radio, No Smoking Sections on commercial aircraft, etc. If you would like to learn more about ASH or to make a tax-free contribution write: Ash/Action on Smoking & Health, P. O. Box 19556, Washington, D. C. 20006.

October 18, 1975 *The Boston Globe*

There may soon be on the market a new type of cigarette created by a Beacon Hill inventor named Richard R. Walton. Reports indicate that the Walton cigarette has an outer paper wrap, and under it a corrugated paper wrap. There is a corrugated plug at the mouth end. Normally, as a cigarette is smoked, the unburned tobacco collects tar and nicotine from the smoke passing through it. As the cigarette burns shorter, the smoke contains higher and higher levels of tar and nicotine. In the Walton, by drawing all the smoke through the corrugated openings along the sides, the unburned tobacco is collecting no extra tar and nicotine. The first and last puff are the same. This would be a major advancement towards making safer cigarettes.

In August 1971, there appeared on the market a new cigarette modestly titled Triumph. Some of the ad copy went as follows: "Newly blended, super mild Triumph Smokes contain no tobacco and no nicotine. Triumphs look and smoke like cigarettes but contain no tobacco." They came in regular and menthol, were on the market for a few months, never told what they were made of, and evidently sold so poorly that they have not been heard from since.

March 29, 1976 *Moneysworth*

"SMOKERS' SOCIAL LIVES NOW IN ASHES"
by Georgia Dullea (N. Y. Times News Service)

Warning: Cigarette smoking is hazardous to your social standing.

Today, more than a decade after the Surgeon General branded smoking as unhealthy, it is finally becoming unfashionable in some circles, unconscionable in others.

Despite a rise in per capita cigarette consumption and a nation of 52 million smokers, some hostesses now equate ashtrays with spittoons when it comes to coffee-table chic.

The message — often unspoken but instantly sensed by the guest who blithely flicks his Bic only to find no place to flick his ashes — "Yes, I mind if you smoke."

"I have some dear friends I booze with once a week," a fortyish woman says. "I am forced to go and get the ashtray from their kitchen closet and I resent that."

All this delights the anti-smoking groups. As they see it, a self-conscious smoker may eventually become a self-motivated quitter.

"Social pressure against smoking seems to be a new trend. We're watching it closely here," says Beverly Schwartz, a spokesman for the National Interagency Council on Smoking and Health, a coalition of 33 government and private groups ranging from the United States Public Health Service to the American Cancer Society.

"They tell me it's becoming uncool to smoke," Ms. Schwartz says, sounding a bit surprised. "It's considered more cool now to say, 'I'm strong, I'm super-independent, I don't need a cigarette any more.' This is the new thing."

June 1975 *Wall Street Journal*
This report from the *Journal* once again reflects Congress' cowardly reluctance to show concern for the citizen over the corporation. "The House Commerce Committee voted to make the Consumer Product Safety Commission keep its hands off bullets and cigarettes. What's more, the committee rejected, 17 to 11, a proposal to give the commission jurisdiction over cigarettes as a fire hazard, if not a health hazard."

July 1975 *Free Press,* Detroit
EX-CIGARETTE SMOKERS FOUND TO INHALE CIGAR SMOKE: So you thought you'd play it safe and switch from cigarettes to cigars? You may only have increased the hazard to your health, says a University of South Florida chest physician. Dr. Allen L. Goldman says that for most cigarette smokers inhaling has become so natural that they can't unlearn the habit, and they end up inhaling cigar smoke. According to a report in the *Journal of the American Medical Association*, Goldman compared the results of inhaling cigarettes and cigar smoke and found that inhaling cigar smoke might actually be more dangerous.

February 11, 1976 *New York Post*
"17 AND UNDER, 39% PUFF A PACK A DAY"
This incorrect headline comes from a recently released survey from the American Cancer Society. The study was done by Yankelovich, Skelly and White. What it actually said was that among those 17 and

under, 27% smoke. Of these, 39% go through a pack or more a day. In other words, 10½% of the 17-year olds and under smoke a pack or more a day.

The alarming news from this study is the fact that 27% of these young people are smokers, and this is *up* from 22% in 1969. 60% of these young smokers said they began before age 13. Among women 18 to 35, the smoking rate is an unhealthy 36% with 61% doing a pack a day or more.

March 1967 *Boston Globe*
"TEENAGE SMOKERS ENGAGE IN
MORE SEX, STUDY SHOWS"

This headline wasn't exactly what the American Cancer Society had in mind when they released several studies by Yankelovich, Skelly and White. Outside of a few religious persuasions, no one has suggested: "Warning: it has been determined that sex is dangerous to your health." The thrust of these studies was the increase in teenage smoking and their attitude that the dangers of smoking were exaggerated.

However, to confirm the *Globe* headline, the surveys found that 57% of the teenage boy smokers reported engaging in sexual intercourse compared to only 23% of the non-smoking boys. 31% of the girls who smoked said they had sex compared to 8% of the non-smokers.

May 10, 1976 *Advertising Age*
"Paris — The French government plans to ban tobacco advertising on TV, radio and at movie theaters, while allowing print ads to carry only the brand name and trademark. Health Minister Simone Veil said the government's goal is not to sharply reduce the use of

tobacco, but to discourage young people from starting to smoke."

June 1975

The Swedish government is trying to discourage smoking by making it a more and more expensive habit. The cost of a pack today is nearly $1.50, and the government plans to gradually increase this to over $3.00. This will cost a two-pack-a-day smoker more than $2,000 a year. Even the cost of killing oneself is getting out of hand.

Question: If, instead of spending a modest 50 cents a day for cigarettes you invested this amount in a savings bank at 6% interest compounded daily, how much money would be in your account after 47 years?
Answer: $47,991.86

Many people who quit, regularly deposit the money saved in a special savings account. This can run from $20 to $60 a month.

May 18, 1976 Associated Press

The Federal Trade Commission yesterday asked Congress to make it a law that all cigarette packages carry the following new and stronger warning: "Cigarette smoking is dangerous to health, and may cause death from cancer, coronary heart disease, chronic bronchitis, pulmonary emphysema and other diseases."

March 1976 News Release from State Mutual Life Assurance Company of America

In January 1964, the United States Surgeon General's report on smoking and health was published. Three months later, State Mutual offered the first non-smoker discounts on life insurance. Twelve years later, their sales of non-smoker life insurance exceeded $2 billion face value, an extraordinary success story. They are happy to point out that, at 65 cents a pack of cigarettes per day, a male age 30 could buy more than $13,000 of non-smoker whole life insurance, or more than $80,000 of non-smoker yearly renewable term insurance. Since premiums for females are lower, a 30-year-old female could do even better.

State Mutual has recently introduced non-smoker discounts on disability income insurance. An affiliate, Hanover Insurance, pioneered non-smoker discounts on homeowner insurance. Many other insurance companies are considering or now offer similar non-smoker discounts.

June 21, 1975 *News,* Bangor, Maine
The Maine Lung Association reported that Maine led the way when it banned smoking in public places in 1848 — 127 years ago. If a clearly legible "No Smoking" sign was posted near each principal entrance, persons were prohibited from entering "any mill, millyard, factory, machine shop, shipyard, covered bridge, stable or other building with a lighted pipe or cigar." The law, which still stands, was amended to include cigarettes in 1939.

May 1975
Secretary of Agriculture, Earl Butz, one of President Ford's less successful appointees, declared that the to-

Tiny puffs contentedly on one of the several cigarettes his owner says the terrier smokes each day. Ray Harless of Franklin, Ind., says Tiny even enjoys an occasional cigar. The dog, Harless claims, begs and whines whenever he feels like a smoke. (UPI)

bacco industry should be thankful for the warning which is printed on every pack of cigarettes because "every time they put it on, the consumption goes up." He added, "As long as tobacco is not declared illegal — and it has not been yet — we're going to be doing everything possible in this department (agriculture) to keep this industry healthy."

June 1975

"Fumes or Famine" might describe a new point of view on tobacco crops and world starvation. The U.S. Department of Agriculture estimates that 10.5 million acres were planted to tobacco worldwide in 1974. The U.S., second only to China, used 963,000 acres for this crop. What would the yield be if the U.S. acreage were switched to —

Corn	1,900,000 tons
Wheat	791,000 tons
Oats	715,000 tons
Soybeans	679,000 tons

As fertilizer costs skyrocket and population growth strains the world's agricultural resources, the wisdom of expending large amounts of energy to harvest a non-nutritional crop may come under increasing attack.

March 1976 *California Farmer,* San Francisco

Dr. Harold Daniell of Redding has photographed the faces of more than 1,000 cigarette smokers, compared them with photos of non-smokers, and concluded that smokers' wrinkles are far more prominent and numerous than non-smokers' of the same age and sex.

November 1975 *Jewish Advocate,* Boston

Next week more than 1,000 people will graduate from a SmokEnders seminar. With over 100,000 graduates successfully completing the program, SmokEnders has become the number one living force in creating a nonsmoking epidemic in this country with chapters coast-to-coast and in Toronto, Canada. "The message of health has been too long played upon by the nonsmoking enthusiasts," says Dan Verrico, Area Sponsor for SmokEnders. "That is why SmokEnders does not employ scare tactics in its presentation. There are aspects of quitting smoking that are quite practical."

A non-smoker can save money, have more stamina, and gain freedom and self-respect. "It's interesting," Verrico went on to say, "how smokers never look like the ads depict them." Most efforts by governmental agencies have failed because of a general unilateral approach to the problem. SmokEnders approaches the problem on all levels — physical, psychological, social and automatic. It is this approach, along with its technology, efficacy and integrity, that has made SmokEnders the leader in its field for the past seven years.

July 1975

Andrews University audiologist, Stephen Prescod, says there is a definite link between heavy smoking and loss of hearing. Prescod reports that "smoking can affect one's hearing in much the same way that aging does. Those smoking 20 or more cigarettes a day can expect enough loss in sensitivity to both high and low frequencies to impair understanding of normal speech."

July 1975 *Buffalo Evening News*

If you're a non-smoker, every cigarette a smoker lights up may be money out of your pocket. "More than 10 percent of all hospital and medical expenses in the United States are tobacco related," a public educator from Roswell Park Memorial Institute said today. In the end, this raises the cost of everybody's health insurance, Russell C. Sciandra told 30 participants in Buffalo State's University College Workshop on Smoking and Health. "We're all paying for a smoker's self-inflicted disease."

March 1976 *Newsleader,* Richmond, Virginia

The tobacco industry is coming under increasing fire from "anti-tobacco zealots," and must prepare to fight back, Virginia leaf producers have been told.

If the industry fails to fight for its interests, tobacco farmers were warned, they stand to lose their price support system, smokers will be discriminated against and cigarettes will be taxed according to tar and nicotine content.

One of the visiting officials was Bill Anderson, executive director of the Tobacco Growers Information Bureau in Raleigh, N. C.

Declaring no constituent of cigarettes is harmful to human health, Anderson said: "I don't apologize for nicotine. It's what brings repeat business. It's what makes people come back."

The meeting was held in the Chatham Educational and Cultural Center auditorium, where smoking is not allowed and ashtrays are not available.

April 1976 *North Penn Reporter*, Lansdale, Pennsylvania
"UP IN SMOKE"

Smokers in this country puff nearly 40 tons of solid pollution into the air each day in the form of smoke particles, Dr. Thomas Mulvany of the Harvard Medical School reports. He cites a further example of smokers' pollution — the butts and wrappers of the 80 million packs of cigarettes smoked daily in the United States. This adds up to about 1,760 tons of trash, not counting cartons and shipping boxes. Is the habit really worth all that?

January 1977 *Canadian Council on Smoking and Health*
"SMOKING GRAIN!"

R.J. Reynolds is experimenting with the use of grain as "tobacco extender." Their results to date indicate a possible lowering of "tar" and nicotine levels "without reducing smoker satisfaction or altering tobacco taste." The grains involved include corn, wheat, rice and millet. The process involves shredding these cereal grains and combining them with various amounts of tobacco, into a smoking mixture.

April 1976 *Capital Journal*, Salem, Oregon
"SMOKE COSTLY"

A lung disease largely caused by cigarette smoking costs an estimated $1.5 billion in doctor and hospital

DOONESBURY
by Garry Trudeau

Copyright 1977 G.B. Trudeau /distributed by Universal Press Syndicate.

bills and lost earnings in 1970, a Blue Cross Association study showed today.

The study suggested the government compare the total costs of smoking-related illnesses with revenues it obtains from the tobacco industry.

Pulmonary emphysema, second leading cause of disability among American workers after heart disease, was the subject of study. It is one of the diseases for which cigarette smoking is most strongly blamed.

March 1976 *States-Item*, New Orleans, Louisiana
"TOBACCO AD BAN GOES UP IN SMOKE"

Norway's total ban on cigarette and tobacco advertising, in force since July, 1975, seems to have had little effect on smoking.

32% of women aged 16 or over now smoke, as do 49% of men. Both figures are about the same as a year ago.

July 1977, Associated Press
SOCHI, USSR — Smoking is still a popular vice in the Soviet Union's first "no-smoking city," but anti-smoking campaigners haven't given up.

One year after the campaign was launched, many citizens of this Black Sea resort 850 miles south of Moscow seem slightly embarrassed by the whole thing.

Out-of-town visitors are met with polite invitations to smoke if they wish to, but to be discreet about it.

Driving from the airport past a sign saying "Welcome to Sochi — Please Don't Smoke," a taxi driver invites his passenger to have a cigarette, "but please just hold it down so no one sees it."

Although restaurants have no-smoking signs, and ash trays are not placed on the tables, smokers are tolerated. In some cases, restaurants are even more lenient than in Moscow, where a new anti-smoking ordinance in restaurants is having some effect.

But Dr. Vladimir Sarmakeshev, a leader in the Sochi campaign, refuses to be discouraged.

"This is not the work of one day or one year," he said. "This is a continuous job. We mustn't be disappointed by the early results. We must find new means."

1976
National Clearinghouse for Smoking and Health (H.E.W.)

According to the report on "Adult Use of Tobacco" in the United States, 9 out of 10 smokers have tried to quit smoking or probably would try if they could find an easy way to do it. They go on smoking even though at least 7 out of 10 are worried about the effect on their health.

June 1977, *Moneysworth*
"CHEWS YOUR POISON"

Nicotine-laced chewing gum may become available as an alternative for smokers who want to quit but can't go "cold turkey." The American Journal of Psychiatry reports that researchers have been able to get two-pack-a-day smokers off the weed in three weeks without nicotine withdrawal symptoms such as anxiety and decreased alertness. In experiments, smokers were weaned from nicotine starting with packages of gum containing 4 milligrams of the toxic substance per stick. In successive stages they were moved to gum containing 3 milligrams, then 2, and so on. Nicotine gum has been available in Sweden for several years and reportedly has proved an effective aid to kicking the habit.

1977
Norway's per capita consumption of cigarettes is the lowest in the world, 615 per year or 1.7 per day. The United States average is the world's highest, 3,321 or 10.5 per day.

1935 *Fortune Magazine*
Smoking in church used to be common, and the first edict *against* tobacco came from Pope Urban VIII in 1642, who forbade it because of the noise set up by steel and flint among echoing naves during Mass.

1976
If a cigarette brand can achieve a 1% share of the total market, it translates to $80,000,000 in sales at the factory. In 1976, 18 new cigarette brands were introduced, and 12 of these were in the "low tar" category. The most successful was Merit which appeared in January 1976. In less than 18 months, with the help of about

$40,000,000 in advertising, it had captured a 2.2% share of the market which indicates a factory sales level of $176,000,000. It is interesting to note that Carlton, which has been around for about 20 years, and is now at the very lowest 1 mg. tar level, has a very respectable 1% share of the market.

June 1977 *Moneysworth*
"CHEWS YOUR POISON"
Nicotine-laced chewing gum may become available as an alternative for smokers who want to quit but can't go "cold turkey." The American Journal of Psychiatry reports that researchers have been able to get two-pack-a-day smokers off the weed in three weeks without nicotine withdrawal symptoms such as anxiety and decreased alertness. In experiments, smokers were weaned from nicotine starting with packages of gum containing 4 milligrams of the toxic substance per stick. In successive stages they were moved to gum containing 3 milligrams, then 2, and so on. Nicotine gum has been available in Sweden for several years and reportedly has proved an effective aid to kicking the habit.

July 1977 *Moneysworth*
Growing up in smoke can be dangerous to the health of houseplants, California plant pathologist Dennis Mayhew advises. A hard-to-kill virus called tobacco mosaic can be spread via the hands and clothing of cigarette-smoking gardeners, and once the virus strikes there is no cure. So, if you've got a green thumb

and tobacco-stained fingers, wash your hands or wear gloves when handling your plants.

1938 *N.Y. World Telegram*

Cigarettes giving off smoke of any hue — blood red to match red fingernails or lips, or any color of the rainbow to match gowns or jewelry — may soon be had. U.S. Patent No. 2,094,614 has been granted Otto L. Miller on a process for treating cigarettes to give off colored smoke.

March 1976 *Journal of the American Dental Association*

"The cigarette smoking habits of people in some parts of the world include a variation called reverse smoking, which is accomplished by holding the lighted end of a cigarette or cigar inside the mouth. Air is drawn to the burning zone through the unlighted end of a cigarette, and smoke is expelled back through the cigarette or out through the mouth. The smoke is not usually inhaled; however, the ashes are swallowed. Reverse smoking has been reported to occur in the lower economic groups in areas of India, the Caribbean, Sardinia, South America, Korea, and the Philippine Islands. In the Philippine Islands, reverse smoking is referred to as "bakwe" and is practiced almost exclusively by married women. Reverse smokers give several reasons for indulging in this peculiar habit: it is more pleasurable than conventional smoking; it gives one the feeling of warmth during the rainy season."

Copyright 1976 by Herblock in The Washington Post.

October 1976 *American Lung Association Bulletin*

"For almost two years, the tobacco industry has conducted a well-financed campaign to discredit opponents of second-hand smoke and to cast doubts on the scientific evidence linking smoking and disease. This is a well-orchestrated public relations effort, composed with skill and performed with talent. From the beginning, the American Lung Association has been singled out as a target. William F. Dwyer, assistant to the president of the Tobacco Institute, suggested to broadcasters and editors that there was 'another side' to the smoking and health story. Soon, he was joined by Connie Drath, a pretty blonde and a non-smoker, who sometimes supported his performance, sometimes appeared on her own. Dwyer and Drath were able to place themselves on local radio and TV interview shows, and eventually on the ABC and NBC television networks. Since early in 1974, Drath and Dwyer made more than 500 single or joint appearances on radio, television and before the public and press in 32 states in what has to be the most successful media blitz ever launched by the tobacco industry. They insist that courtesy, not legislation is the solution for those who are annoyed by smoke in public places, and they deny the existence — even the possibility — of a health hazard. Lung associations have scheduled press conferences immediately after those called by Tobacco Institute speakers, frequently next door. Reporters have covered both."

1977 *ASH Newsletter*

"Michigan, which recently passed a new law modeled in part on the Minnesota Clean Indoor Air Act, requires restaurants seating more than 50 to provide separate sections for non-smokers."

"A special tea, made from roasted, dried tea leaves, is inspiring some Japanese smokers to abandon cigarettes because they suddenly taste bad. Marketed as 'quit-smoking tea,' the product is bitter and brown and reportedly shifts the drinker's body from acidity to alkalinity. No scientific explanation has been given for the fact that 40% of the smokers have quit, and others have drastically reduced their consumption."

"When the Surgeon General's report was issued in 1964 providing clear evidence of the link between smoking and disease, more than 30 per cent of all physicians were smokers. In the ensuing 13 years, that proportion has been cut by one-third, with 21 per cent of doctors still puffing, according to the National Clearinghouse for Smoking and Health in Atlanta. Other health professionals, including dentists and pharmacists, also have given up smoking in droves. Nurses, however, have not been equally successful in quitting, the Clearinghouse survey showed."

BIBLIOGRAPHY

Allen, William A., Gerhard Angermann, William A. Fackler. "Learning to Live Without Cigarettes." Dolphin Books, Doubleday and Co., Inc. 1968

Beer, George Lewis. "The Origins of the British Colonial System 1578-1660." Gloucester, Mass., P. S. Smith 1959

Brean, Herbert. "How to Stop Smoking." The Vanguard Press 1959; Pocket Book Edition 1975

Brecher, Ruth. "The Consumers Union Report on Smoking and the Public Interest." Consumers Union 1963

Cain, Arthur H. "Young People and Smoking; The Use and Abuse of Cigarette Tobacco." J. Day Co. 1964

Corti, Egon Caesar. "A History of Smoking." Harcourt, Brace & Co. 1932

Danysh, Joseph. "Stop Without Quitting." 1974. International Society for General Semantics, P. O. Box 2469, San Francisco, CA 94126

Diehl, Harold S. "Tobacco and Your Health: The Smoking Controversy." McGraw-Hill Book Co. 1969

Drayton, William Jr. "The Tar and Nicotine Tax." The Yale Law Journal, Volume 81, Number 8, July 1972

Fort, Joel. "The Pleasure Seekers: The Drug Crisis, Youth and Society." The Bobbs-Merrill Co. 1969

Fritschler, A. Lee. "Smoking and Politics; Policymaking and the Federal Bureaucracy." Appleton-Century-Crofts 1969

Madis, George. "Smoking, Life and Health: How and Why to Stop Smoking." American Book Pub. Co. 1964

Mausner, Bernard. "Smoking! A Behavioral Analysis." Pergamon Press 1971

Neuberger, Maurine B. "Smoke Screen: Tobacco and the Public Welfare." Prentice 1963

Osborn, Robert and Fred W. Benton, M.D. "Dying to Smoke." Houghton Mifflin Co. 1964

United States Surgeon General's Advisory Committee on Smoking and Health. U. S. Govt. Printing Office 1964

Vermes, Jean Cambell (Pattison). "Pot is Rot, and other Horrible Facts About Bad Things." N. Y. Association Press 1969

Wagner, Susan. "Cigarette Country." Praeger Publishers 1971

REPORT OF "TAR" AND NICOTINE CONTENT OF THE SMOKE OF 166 VARIETIES OF CIGARETTES
June 1977

The Federal Trade Commission's Laboratory has determined the "tar" (dry particulate matter) and total alkaloid (reported as nicotine) content of 166 varieties of cigarettes. The laboratory utilized the Cambridge filter method with the following specifications as set forth in the Commission's announcement of July 31, 1967:

1. Smoke cigarettes to a 23 mm. butt length, or to the length of the filter and overwrap plus 3 mm. if in excess of 23 mm.
2. Base results on a test of 95 cigarettes per brand, or type.
3. Cigarettes to be tested will be selected on a random basis, as opposed to "weight selection."
4. Determine particulate matter on a "dry" basis employing the gas chromatography method published by C. H. Sloan and B. J. Sublett in Tobacco Science 9, page 70, 1965, as modified by F. J. Schultz' and A. W. Spears' report published in

Tobacco, Vol. 162, No. 24, page 32, dated June 17, 1966, to determine the moisture content.

5. Determine and report the "tar" content after subtracting moisture and alkaloids (as nicotine) from particulate matter.

Concerning the 166 varieties tested, 23 were capable of being smoked to 23 mm. The butt length of the other 143 varieties tested ranged from 25.0 mm. to an average of between 47.7 and 49.5. The butt lengths of 102 of the 166 varieties tested exceeded 30 mm.

The samples used were obtained by attempting to purchase two packages of each variety of cigarettes as distributed by the 7 domestic cigarette manufacturers during November 1976 in each of 50 geographic locations throughout the country. All varieties of cigarettes were not available in each of the 50 geographic locations and in these instances, one or more additional packages of cigarettes were purchased in those geographic locations where respective varieties were available. The samples utilized in the tests were representative of the 166 varieties of cigarettes as available throughout the country at the time of purchase.

In the Table listing the cigarette varieties in alphabetical order, the "tar" content is reported to the nearest 1/10 milligram and the nicotine to the nearest 1/100 milligram, each with appropriate statistical values. The average weight is reported in grams per cigarette and the butt length range to the nearest 1/10 millimeter. In all other tables the average weight and butt length columns and the figures representing the standard deviation of the mean have been eliminated.

REPORT OF "TAR" AND NICOTINE CONTENT OF THE SMOKE OF 166 VARIETIES OF CIGARETTES
June 1977

ALPHABETICAL LISTING BY BRAND NAME
Listing of "Tar"[1] Values for Five (5) Testing Periods

BRAND	TYPE	Mar. 1975	Sept. 1975	Apr. 1976	Nov. 1976	June 1977
Alpine	king size, filter, menthol	13	14	14	15	14
Alpine	100 mm, filter, menthol, (hard pack)	16	*	*	*	*
American Lights	120 mm, filter	*	*	*	*	8
American Lights	120 mm, filter, menthol	*	*	*	*	10
American Longs	120 mm, filter	*	*	*	21	16
American Longs	120 mm, filter, menthol	*	*	*	17	16
Belair	king size, filter, menthol	15	15	15	15	15
Belair	100 mm, filter, menthol	17	17	17	18	18
Benson & Hedges	reg. size, filter, (hard pack)	9	9	9	10	10
Benson & Hedges	king size, filter, (hard pack)	16	16	16	16	16
Benson & Hedges 100's	100 mm, filter, (hard pack)	*	*	*	17	17
Benson & Hedges 100's	100 mm, filter, menthol, (hard pack)	*	*	*	17	17
Benson & Hedges 100's	100 mm, filter	17	18	18	18	17
Benson & Hedges 100's	100 mm, filter, menthol	17	18	18	18	17
Bull Durham	king size, filter	28	29	29	30	29
Camel	reg. size, non-filter	25	23	24	23	25
Camel	king size, filter, (hard pack)	*	*	18	19	19
Camel Filters	king size, filter	19	19	18	19	18
Capri	110 mm, filter	*	*	18	*	*
Capri	110 mm, filter, menthol	*	*	19	*	*
Carlton 70's	reg. size, filter	2	2	2	<0.5	<0.5
Carlton	king size, filter	4	4	4	1	1
Carlton	king size, filter, menthol	4	4	4	1	1
Chesterfield	reg. size, non-filter	24	24	25	25	24
Chesterfield	king size, non-filter	29	28	28	28	29
Chesterfield	king size, filter	18	19	19	19	19
Chesterfield	king size, filter, menthol	19	19	*	*	*
Chesterfield	101 mm, filter	20	19	20	18	18
Dawn	120 mm, filter	*	*	24	21	*
Dawn	120 mm, filter, menthol	*	*	24	22	*
Domino	king size, non-filter	26	29	30	31	33
Domino	king size, filter	23	24	24	23	21
Doral	king size, filter	15	14	15	13	12
Doral	king size, filter, menthol	13	13	14	11	11
DuMaurier	king size, filter, (hard pack)	15	16	15	16	16
Eagle 20's	king size, filter	*	*	*	19	18
Eagle 20's	king size, filter, menthol	*	*	*	19	18
English Ovals	reg. size, non-filter, (hard pack)	22	22	23	24	24
English Ovals	king size, non-filter, (hard pack)	29	29	29	29	30
Eve	100 mm, filter	19	19	18	17	16
Eve	100 mm, filter, menthol	19	18	19	17	16
Eve 120's	120 mm, filter, (hard pack)	*	*	*	14	15
Eve 120's	120 mm, filter, menthol, (hard pack)	*	*	*	15	14
Fact	king size, filter, menthol	*	*	*	14	13
Fact	king size, filter, menthol	*	*	*	13	13
Fatima	king size, non-filter	28	28	27	28	29
Galaxy	king size, filter	15	15	16	16	15
Half & Half	king size, filter	25	25	25	25	26
Hallmark	100 mm, filter, (hard pack)	*	*	*	*	23
Hallmark	100 mm, filter, menthol, (hard pack)	*	*	*	*	23
Herbert Tareyton	king size, non-filter	29	29	28	28	28
Hi-Lite	100 mm, filter, (hard pack)	*	*	*	*	11
Home Run	reg. size, non-filter	21	20	20	21	22
Iceberg 100's	100 mm, filter, menthol	9	9	9	9	3

Kent	king size, filter, (hard pack)	15	15	15	16	15
Kent	king size, filter	16	16	16	17	16
Kent Golden Lights	king size, filter	*	*	*	9	8
Kent Golden Lights	king size, filter, menthol	*	*	*	*	8
Kent	100 mm, filter	19	18	18	18	18
Kent	100 mm, filter, menthol	18	17	17	17	17
King Sano	king size, filter	8	7	7	7	6
King Sano	king size, filter, menthol	7	7	8	7	6
Kool	reg. size, non-filter, menthol	19	20	20	20	21
Kool	king size, filter, menthol, (hard pack)	16	17	17	18	17
Kool Naturals	king size, filter	*	*	*	*	14
Kool	king size, filter, menthol	16	17	17	17	17
Kool Milds	king size, filter, menthol	13	13	13	14	14

* Denotes varieties not available during market sampling

[1]TPM dry (tar) - milligrams total particulate matter less nicotine and water

BRAND	TYPE	Tar (mg/cig)	Nicotine (mg/cig)
Benson & Hedges	king size, filter, (hard pack)	16	1.0
Long Johns	120 mm, filter, menthol	16	1.3
Eve	100 mm, filter	16	1.0
Virginia Slims	100 mm, filter	16	0.9
Pall Mall	100 mm, filter, menthol	16	1.2
Eve	100 mm, filter, menthol	16	1.0
Silva Thins	100 mm, filter, menthol	16	1.1
Tall	120 mm, filter, menthol	16	1.3
Saratoga	120 mm, filter, (hard pack)	16	1.0
American Longs	120 mm, filter	16	1.3
L & M	king size, filter, (hard pack)	16	0.9
Raleigh	king size, filter	16	1.1
American Longs	120 mm, filter, menthol	16	1.3
Philip Morris International	100 mm, filter, (hard pack)	16	1.0
Philip Morris International	100 mm, filter, menthol, (hard pack)	16	0.9
Tareyton	100 mm, filter	16	1.2
Marlboro	100 mm, filter, (hard pack)	17	1.0
Benson & Hedges 100's	100 mm, filter, (hard pack)	17	1.0
Benson & Hedges 100's	100 mm, filter, menthol	17	1.0
Marlboro	king size, filter, (hard pack)	17	1.0
Marlboro	100 mm, filter	17	1.0
Silva Thins	100 mm, filter	17	1.3
Kent	100 mm, filter, menthol	17	1.1
St. Moritz	100 mm, filter	17	1.0
Old Gold Filters	king size, filter, (hard pack)	17	1.2
Benson & Hedges 100's	100 mm, filter	17	1.0
Twist	100 mm, lemon/menthol	17	1.3
Kool	king size, filter, menthol, (hard pack)	17	1.3
Kool	king size, filter, menthol	17	1.3
Max	120 mm, filter, menthol	17	1.3
Tareyton	king size, filter	17	1.2
Marlboro	king size, filter	17	1.0
Benson & Hedges 100s	100 mm, filter, menthol, (hard pack)	17	1.1
St. Moritz	100 mm, filter, menthol	17	1.1
Max	120 mm, filter	17	1.3
L & M	100 mm, filter	17	1.1
Newport	king size, filter, menthol, (hard pack)	17	1.2
Raleigh	100 mm, filter	17	1.2
Newport	king size, filter, menthol	17	1.2
Sano	reg. size, non-filter	18	0.6
Lark	king size, filter	18	1.1
Montclair	king size, filter, menthol	18	1.3
Kool	100 mm, filter, menthol	18	1.3
Pall Mall	king size, filter	18	1.2
L & M	100 mm, filter, menthol	18	1.1
Old Gold Filters	king size, filter	18	1.2
Viceroy	100 mm, filter	18	1.3
Salem	king size, filter, menthol	18	1.2
Belair	100 mm, filter, menthol	18	1.3
Long Johns	120 mm, filter	18	1.4
Chesterfield	101 mm, filter	18	1.1
Camel Filters	king size, filter	18	1.2
Tall	120 mm, filter	18	1.4
L & M	king size, filter	18	1.1
Winston	100 mm, filter, menthol	18	1.2
Kent	100 mm, filter	18	1.2
Eagle 20's	king size, filter	18	1.1
Eagle 20's	king size, filter, menthol	18	1.1
Lark	100 mm, filter	18	1.1
Salem	100 mm, filter, menthol	18	1.3
Salem	king size, filter, menthol, (hard pack)	19	1.2
Winston	king size, filter, (hard pack)	19	1.2

BRAND	TYPE	Tar (mg/cig)	Nicotine (mg/cig)
Winston	king size, filter	19	1.2
Spring 100's	100 mm, filter, menthol	19	1.1
Chesterfield	king size, filter	19	1.1
Pall Mall	100 mm, filter	19	1.4
Oasis	king size, filter, menthol	19	1.1
Winston	100 mm, filter	19	1.3
L.T. Brown	120 mm, filter	19	1.5
L.T. Brown	120 mm, filter, menthol	19	1.4
Camel	king size, filter, (hard pack)	19	1.2
Newport	100 mm, filter, menthol	20	1.4
Old Gold Straights	reg. size, non-filter	20	1.2
Philip Morris	reg. size, non-filter	20	1.1
More	120 mm, filter	21	1.5
Kool	reg. size, non-filter, menthol	21	1.3
More	120 mm, filter, menthol	21	1.6
Old Gold 100's	100 mm, filter	21	1.4
Picayune	reg. size, non-filter	21	1.4
Domino	king size, filter	21	1.1
Home Run	reg. size, non-filter	22	1.5
Hallmark	100 mm, filter, menthol, (hard pack)	23	1.8
Stratford	king size, filter	23	1.1
Mapleton	king size, filter	23	1.2
Hallmark	100 mm, filter, (hard pack)	23	1.9
English Ovals	reg. size, non-filter	24	1.6
Piedmont	reg. size, non-filter	24	1.3
Raleigh	king size, non-filter	24	1.4
Chesterfield	reg. size, non-filter	24	1.4
Lucky Strike	reg. size, non-filter	24	1.4
Philip Morris Commander	king size, non-filter	24	1.4
Old Gold Straights	king size, non-filter	25	1.5
Camel	reg. size, non-filter	25	1.6
Pall Mall	king size, non-filter	26	1.6
Half & Half	king size, filter	26	1.8
Mapleton	reg. size, non-filter	28	1.3
Herbert Tareyton	king size, non-filter	28	1.8
Stratford	king size, non-filter	29	1.1
Fatima	king size, non-filter	29	1.7
Bull Durham	king size, filter	29	1.9
Chesterfield	king size, non-filter	29	1.7
English Ovals	king size, non-filter, (hard pack)	30	2.1
Domino	king size, non-filter	33	1.4
Players	reg. size, non-filter, (hard pack)	34	2.5

Listing of "Tar"[1] Values for Five (5) Testing Periods

BRAND	TYPE	Mar. 1975	Sept. 1975	Apr. 1976	Nov. 1976	June 1977
Phoenix	120 mm, filter, menthol	*	*	*	19	*
Picayune	reg. size, non-filter	20	20	20	20	21
Piedmont	reg. size, non-filter	25	25	24	24	24
Players	reg. size, non-filter, (hard pack)	31	31	31	32	34
Raleigh	king size, non-filter	24	22	24	24	24
Raleigh	king size, filter	16	16	16	16	16
Raleigh Lights	king size, filter	*	*	*	*	14
Raleigh	100 mm, filter	17	17	17	18	17
Raleigh Extra Mild	king size, filter	14	13	14	14	*
St. Moritz	100 mm, filter	17	18	18	18	17
St. Moritz	100 mm, filter, menthol	18	18	18	18	17
Safari	100 mm, filter	19	19	20	*	*
Salem	king size, filter, menthol, (hard pack)	19	19	19	19	19
Salem	king size, filter, menthol	19	19	19	18	18
Salem Extra	king size, filter, menthol	18	17	*	*	*
Salem Lights	king size, filter, menthol	*	*	*	11	11
Salem	100 mm, filter, menthol	19	19	19	18	18
Salem Long Lights	100 mm, filter, menthol	*	*	*	*	9
Sano	reg. size, non-filter	22	18	18	18	18
Saratoga	120 mm, filter, (hard pack)	*	17	18	16	16
Saratoga	120 mm, filter, menthol, (hard pack)	*	15	18	16	15
Silva Thins	100 mm, filter	17	17	17	17	17
Silva Thins	100 mm, filter, menthol	16	16	16	16	16
Spring 100's	100 mm, filter, menthol	21	20	19	19	19
Stratford	king size, non-filter	*	*	*	27	29
Stratford	king size, filter	*	*	*	25	23
Super M	100 mm, filter, menthol	17	17	16	17	*
Tall	120 mm, filter	*	*	*	20	18
Tall	120 mm, filter, menthol	*	*	*	17	16
Tareyton	king size, filter	20	21	21	20	17
Tareyton	100 mm, filter	19	20	19	19	16
Tempo	king size, filter	11	11	11	8	7
Tramps	king size, filter	18	17	17	*	*
Tramps	king size, filter, menthol	16	16	16	*	*
True	king size, filter	11	11	11	5	5
True	king size, filter, menthol	12	11	11	6	5
True 100's	100 mm, filter	13	13	12	13	13
True 100's	100 mm, filter, menthol	13	13	13	13	13
Twist	100 mm, filter, lemon/menthol	17	18	18	17	17
Vanguard	king size, filter	*	*	*	15	16
Vanguard	king size, filter, menthol	*	*	*	*	13
Vantage	king size, filter	12	11	11	10	11
Vantage	king size, filter, menthol	11	11	11	11	11
Vello	king size, filter	*	*	*	11	10
Vello	king size, filter, menthol	*	*	*	10	10
Viceroy	king size, filter	16	16	16	16	16
Viceroy Extra Mild	king size, filter	14	14	14	14	14
Viceroy	100 mm, filter	17	17	18	18	18
Virginia Slims	100 mm, filter	17	17	16	16	16
Virginia Slims	100 mm, filter, menthol	17	17	16	16	16
Virginia Slims	120 mm, filter, (hard pack)	*	*	*	16	*
Virginia Slims	120 mm, filter, menthol, (hard pack)	*	*	*	15	*
Winchester	king size, filter	19	*	*	*	*
Winchester	king size, filter, menthol	17	*	*	*	*

Winston	king size, filter, (hard pack)	19	20	18	19	19
Winston	king size, filter	20	20	19	19	19
Winston Lights	king size, filter	14	14	13	13	12
Winston	100 mm, filter	19	18	18	19	19
Winston	100 mm, filter, menthol	19	19	19	19	18
Zack	king size, filter, (hard pack)	*	18	16	18	*
Zack	king size, filter	*	18	18	17	*
Zack	king size, filter, menthol	*	*	17	16	*

* Denotes varieties not available during market sampling

[1]TPM dry (tar) - milligrams total particulate matter less nicotine and water

LISTED BY INCREASING ORDER OF TAR VALUES

BRAND	TYPE	Tar (mg/cig)	Nicotine (mg/cig)
Carlton 70's	reg. size, filter	<0.5	<0.05
Carlton	king size, filter, menthol	1	0.1
Now	king size, filter, menthol, (hard pack)	1	0.1
Carlton	king size, filter	1	0.1
Now	king size, filter, (hard pack)	1	0.1
Iceberg 100's	100 mm, filter, menthol	3	0.3
Lucky 100's	100 mm, filter	3	0.3
True	king size, filter	5	0.4
True	king size, filter, menthol	5	0.4
King Sano	king size, filter	6	0.3
Pall Mall Extra Mild	king size, filter (hard pack)	6	0.5
King Sano	king size, filter	6	0.3
Pall Mall Extra Mild	king size, filter	6	0.5
Tempo	king size, filter	7	0.5
Kent Golden Lights	king size, filter	8	0.6
L & M Lights	king size, filter	8	0.6
Merit	king size, filter, menthol	8	0.5
Merit	king size, filter	8	0.6
Kent Golden Lights	king size, filter, menthol	8	0.7
American Lights	120 mm, filter	8	0.7
Lucky Ten	king size, filter	9	0.6
Salem Long Lights	100 mm, filter, menthol	9	0.7
Parliament	king size, filter, (hard pack)	10	0.6
Benson & Hedges	reg. size, filter, (hard pack)	10	0.6
American Lights	120 mm, filter, menthol	10	0.8
Parliament	king size, filter	10	0.6
Vello	king size, filter, menthol	10	0.7
Vello	king size, filter	10	0.7
Multifilter	king size, filter, menthol	11	0.7
Vantage	king size, filter	11	0.7
Vantage	king size, filter, menthol	11	0.8
Salem Lights	king size, filter, menthol	11	0.8
Doral	king size, filter, menthol	11	0.8
Hi-Lite	100 mm, filter	11	0.7
Marlboro Lights	king size, filter	12	0.7
Parliament	100 mm, filter	12	0.7
Doral	king size, filter	12	0.8
Multifilter	king size, filter	12	0.8
Winston Lights	king size, filter	12	0.9
Fact	king size, filter, menthol	13	0.9
Vanguard	king size, filter, menthol	13	0.9
True 100's	100 mm, filter, menthol	13	0.8
True 100's	100 mm, filter	13	0.8
Fact	king size, filter	13	0.9
Marlboro	king size, filter, menthol	14	0.8
Alpine	king size, filter, menthol	14	0.8
Kool Milds	king size, filter, menthol	14	0.9
Marlboro	king size, filter, menthol, (hard pack)	14	0.8
Raleigh Lights	king size, filter	14	1.0
Viceroy Extra Mild	king size, filter	14	1.0
Eve 120's	120 mm, filter, menthol, (hard pack)	14	1.0
Kool Naturals	king size, filter	14	1.0
Belair	king size, filter, menthol	15	1.0
Galaxy	king size, filter	15	0.9
Eve 120's	120 mm, filter, (hard pack)	15	1.0
Kent	king size, filter, (hard pack)	15	1.0

Saratoga	120 mm, filter, menthol, (hard pack)	15	1.0
Viceroy	king size, filter	16	1.0
DuMaurier	king size, filter, (hard pack)	16	1.1
Vanguard	king size, filter	16	1.0
Virginia Slims	100 mm, filter, menthol	16	0.9
Kent	king size, filter	16	1.0

[1]TPM dry (tar) - milligrams total particulate matter less nicotine and water

Listing of "Tar"[1] Values for Five (5) Testing Periods

BRAND	TYPE	Mar. 1975	Sept. 1975	Apr. 1976	Nov. 1976	June 1977
Kool	100 mm, filter, menthol	17	17	17	18	18
L & M	king size, filter, (hard pack)	18	17	17	17	16
L & M	king size, filter	18	18	19	19	18
L & M Lights	king size, filter	*	*	*	*	8
L & M	100 mm, filter	20	19	19	17	17
L & M	100 mm, filter, menthol	19	20	19	18	18
L.T. Brown	120 mm, filter	*	*	21	20	19
L.T. Brown	120 mm, filter, menthol	*	*	22	19	19
Lark	king size, filter	18	18	18	18	18
Lark	100 mm, filter	19	19	19	19	18
Long Johns	120 mm, filter	*	*	22	18	18
Long Johns	120 mm, filter, menthol	*	*	20	15	16
Lucky Strike	reg. size, non-filter	27	27	26	24	24
Lucky Strike	king size, filter	*	*	*	26	*
Lucky Ten	king size, filter	9	10	9	9	9
Lucky 100's	100 mm, filter	10	10	9	9	3
Mapleton	reg. size, non-filter	30	29	27	27	28
Mapleton	king size, filter	24	23	23	22	23
Marlboro	king size, filter, (hard pack)	17	18	17	17	17
Marlboro	king size, filter, menthol, (hard pack)	13	15	14	14	14
Marlboro	king size, filter	17	18	18	18	17
Marlboro Lights	king size, filter	12	13	13	13	12
Marlboro Lights	king size, filter, menthol	*	13	13	*	*
Marlboro	king size, filter, menthol	14	15	15	14	14
Marlboro	100 mm, filter, (hard pack)	17	17	17	17	17
Marlboro	100 mm, filter	18	17	17	18	17
Max	120 mm, filter	*	*	17	17	17
Max	120 mm, filter, menthol	*	*	17	17	17
Marvels	king size, non-filter	25	*	*	*	*
Marvels	king size, filter	6	*	*	*	*
Marvels	king size, filter, menthol	4	*	*	*	*
Merit	king size, filter	*	*	*	8	8
Merit	king size, filter, menthol	*	*	*	8	8
Miyako	king size, filter	15	14	15	15	*
Montclair	king size, filter, menthol	19	18	19	18	18
More	120 mm, filter	17	21	25	21	21
More	120 mm, filter, menthol	18	21	24	21	21
Multifilter	king size, filter	12	12	13	13	12
Multifilter	king size, filter, menthol	10	10	10	11	11
Newport	king size, filter, menthol, (hard pack)	17	17	16	18	17
Newport	king size, filter, menthol	17	18	17	18	17
Newport	100 mm, filter, menthol	21	19	19	19	20
Now	king size, filter, (hard pack)	*	*	*	1	1
Now	king size, filter, menthol, (hard pack)	*	*	*	1	1
Oasis	king size, filter, menthol	18	18	19	19	19
Old Gold Straights	reg. size, non-filter	20	20	19	19	20
Old Gold Straights	king size, non-filter	24	24	24	23	25
Old Gold Filters	king size, filter, (hard pack)	17	17	16	17	17
Old Gold Filters	king size, filter	18	17	17	17	18
Old Gold 100's	100 mm, filter	23	21	21	21	21
Pall Mall	king size, non-filter	27	28	27	25	26
Pall Mall	king size, filter, (hard pack)	*	*	*	23	*
Pall Mall	king size, filter	*	*	*	18	18
Pall Mall Extra Mild	king size, filter, (hard pack)	9	10	9	7	6
Pall Mall Extra Mild	king size, filter	10	10	10	10	6
Pall Mall	100 mm, filter	20	20	19	19	19

Pall Mall	100 mm, filter, menthol	17	16	16	16	16
Parliament	king size, filter, (hard pack)	14	14	14	15	10
Parliament	king size, filter	15	16	16	15	10
Parliament 100's	100 mm, filter	17	17	17	16	12
Philip Morris	reg. size, non-filter	20	20	19	20	20
Philip Morris Commander	king size, non-filter	25	25	25	24	24
Philip Morris International	100 mm, filter, (hard pack)	17	18	17	18	16
Philip Morris International	100 mm, filter, menthol, (hard pack)	17	16	16	17	16
Phoenix	100 mm, filter, menthol	*	*	*	19	*

* Denotes varieties not available during market sampling

[1]TPM dry (tar) - milligrams total particulate matter less nicotine and water

CANADIAN CIGARETTES
Average "Tar" and Nicotine Contents
Canadian Tobacco Manufacturers' Council

BRAND	TYPE	"Tar"	Nicotine
Alpine	king size, filter, menthol	17	1.3
Belmont	king size, filter, menthol	13	1.1
Belmont	king size, filter	11	0.9
Belmont	reg., filter	7	0.6
Belvedere	king size, filter	17	1.3
Belvedere	king size, filter, menthol	17	1.3
Belvedere	reg., filter	15	1.1
Belvedere	extra mild, king size, filter	11	1.0
Belvedere	extra mild, reg., filter	10	0.8
Benson & Hedges 100's	filter	18	1.4
Benson & Hedges 100's	filter, menthol	18	1.4
Black Cat	reg., plain	18	1.0
Black Cat	reg., cork	18	1.1
Black Cat	reg., filter	14	0.9
British Consols	plain	19	1.2
British Consols	reg., filter	18	1.3
Buckingham	reg., plain	17	0.9
Buckingham	king size, plain	17	1.0
Cameo	king size, filter	18	1.2
Cameo	extra mild, king size, filter	12	0.8
Cavalier	king size, filter	18	1.3
Contessa Slims	king size, filter	13	0.8
Craven "A"	reg., filter	8	0.5
Craven "A"	king size, filter	15	1.0
Craven "A"	king size, filter, menthol	12	0.9
Craven "A" Special Mild	king size, filter	5	0.4
Dudes	king size, filter	19	1.3
Du Maurier	reg., filter	14	0.9
Du Maurier	king size, filter	19	1.3
Du Maurier	king size, filter, menthol	13	0.8
Dumont Select	king size, filter	9	0.6
Dunhill	king size, filter	18	1.2
Embassy	reg., filter	16	1.1
Embassy	king size, filter	19	1.3
Export "A"	reg., filter	18	1.2
Export "A"	king size, filter	19	1.3
Export	plain	19	1.2
Export Lights	reg, filter	14	1.0
Export Lights	king size, filter	14	1.0
Goldcrest 100	filter	15	1.1
John Players Special	king size, filter	16	1.2
Kool	king size, filter	14	0.9
Macdonald	reg., filter, menthol	15	1.0
Macdonald	king size, filter, menthol	16	1.1
Mark Ten	king size, filter	18	1.4
Mark Ten	king size, plain	18	1.3
Mark Ten	king size, filter, menthol	17	1.3
Mark Ten	reg., filter	16	1.2
Mark Ten	reg., plain	15	1.0
Matinée	reg, filter	8	0.5
Matinée	king size, filter	12	0.8
Matinée Special	king size, filter	10	0.7

Brand	Type		
Matinée Special	filter 100's	11	0.8
Maverick	king size, filter	17	1.3
Médaillon	king size, filter	1	0.1
Millbank	king size, filter	19	1.3
Montclair	reg., filter	16	1.2
Montclair	king size, filter	18	1.4
Number 7	king size, filter	18	1.3
Pall Mall	king size, plain	17	1.0
Perilly	king size, filter	16	1.1
Peter Jackson	king size, filter	19	1.3
Peter Stuyvesant	king size, filter	18	1.2
Peter Stuyvesant 100's	filter	16	1.1
Peter Stuyvesant 100's	filter, menthol	16	1.1
Philip Morris	reg., plain	16	0.9
Players	reg., plain	19	1.2
Players Medium	reg., plain	18	1.1
Players	reg., filter	19	1.3
Players	king size, filter	19	1.3
Players Medium	reg., filter	19	1.3
Players No. 6	reg., filter	17	1.2
Players Light	reg., filter	14	0.9
Players Light	king size, filter	17	1.3
Plus	120 mm, filter	19	1.6
Plus	120 mm, filter, menthol	19	1.6
Rothmans	king size, filter	18	1.3
Sportsman	reg., plain	18	1.0
Sportsman	reg., filter	14	0.9
Sportsman	king size, filter	18	1.2
Sweet Caporal	reg., plain	19	1.1
Sweet Caporal	reg., filter	14	0.9
Sweet Caporal	king size, filter	19	1.3
Turret	reg., filter	14	1.0
Turret	king size, filter	18	1.2
Vantage	king size, filter	11	0.8
Viceroy	king size, filter	15	0.9
Viscount	reg., filter	4	0.3
Viscount	king size, filter	5	0.5
Viscount	king size, filter, menthol	5	0.5
Viscount No. 1	Ultra Reg. filter	1	0.1
Viscount No. 1	Ultra Mild king size, filter	1	0.1
Winston	king size, filter	16	1.1